First edition, December 2018

Cover design and photo by author.

Questions or corrections? E-mail the author at:

CallMeTrooper@protonmail.com

Independent Publisher
Copyright © 2018
All rights reserved.
ISBN: 978-1-5323-8905-4
E-Book ISBN: 978-1-5323-8906-1

Call Me
TROOPER

The Chronicles of a
Michigan State Police Officer

Anonymous

This project is written in anonymity:

Each of the officers referred to throughout this book are done so anonymously. I respect each of them and their departments too much to do otherwise.

The officers referenced herein have arrested multitudes. Suspects have been locked up in jails, prisons, and some have been deported as a result of our efforts. Anonymity is therefore also offered as a matter of safety.

I have zero doubt that there are those, who after doing a bit of investigation, can determine the true identity of this author. This is especially so with members of the MSP. Though there are others who could accomplish this as well.

I sincerely request those who, either already have this information, or could gain it; to maintain this anonymity.

Dedication

To my mentors and friends:

The sum of your call sign was 18
Perhaps the hardest charger I ever worked with;
you are also one of the sharpest, most cynical, capable,
and trustworthy men I know.

The sum of your call sign was 24
A warrior, who turned cubs into soldiers, a trooper
who taught rookies how to solve crime.

To my wife
Without your support and assistance,
this project may never have been completed.
Otherwise I remain:
- Speechless -

Preface

What follows is not merely about one trooper.

While each of the narratives describe incidents which
I was involved in; the primary subject is law enforcement.

The majority of the narratives which follow, include references to additional officers. Where I worked, back up was
never far away.

Each of these incidents are true and verifiable. However,
they are presented as examples of some of the types of incidents which police officers might encounter during their careers. They are the heroes, and I was only privileged stand
among their ranks for a time.

The intention of these narratives is *not to imply* that I was
some top tier police officer. I genuinely consider many
coworkers, and officers from other departments, to be
markedly superior to me.

From running in the academy, all the way through to retirement, this trooper was only ever trying to keep up with
those in front.

Table of Contents

"The trooper trusted his instincts, he backed up and quickly escalated to the top of the food chain. My friend knew that circumstances can go from zero to sixty in seconds. He could too."

Chapter One

INTENSITY

WRONG WAY ON THE FREEWAY

Traffic conditions were perfect for running radar, and my ticket book was ready for business. The patrol car was tucked in tight behind a bridge support. It was a favorite fishing hole. On this sunny Michigan afternoon, some un-suspecting lead-foots were about to meet me, and maybe even get my autograph.

The emergency tones sounded over the radio, and the dis-patcher advised that a vehicle was driving the wrong way, eastbound in the three westbound lanes of the freeway. I was two miles east of the call, the driver was headed right in my direction. With emergency lights flashing and siren blar-ing, I tore out of the median towards trouble.

It was only a minute or two before I saw the headlights coming straight at my patrol car. He drove around me and continued the wrong way, in the fast lane. My patrol car spun around as fast as it was designed to do, and the chase was on.

That day, as Murphy's fricken' law would have it, I chose to drive a slick top, (that's a patrol car with no lights on top.) It's great for traffic enforcement but less than stellar for visibility while driving to emergencies.

There was really only one option; pursue him with my emergency lights and siren active in the hopes that I might warn oncoming traffic that this clown was driving directly at them. What else should I have done, let him go smash into a van full of people on their way to see Aunt May? Any decent officer would have made the same choice I did.

Fortunately, it was a stretch of freeway that was straight. I chased him, driving in-between the second and third lanes (middle and fast lanes) hoping that traffic would see my lights around the side of the suspect vehicle; because they sure as hell weren't gonna see any lights coming from above or behind the suspect vehicle. Damn slick tops.

I could see another trooper, driving the same direction as me, but on the correct side of the highway. Not helpful. But then again how many police cars should pursue a suspect the wrong way on a freeway? One is probably prudent.

A few westbound semi-trucks were rather helpful as they had pulled into the fast lane, almost as if to say; if you're gonna hit someone, hit my 80,000-pound truck. They were heroes, driving their big-rigs in the third lane. The suspect swerved onto the shoulder to avoid the oncoming semi-trucks. Once each truck passed, the suspect pulled back into the fast lane, with me on his tail. Apparently, he wasn't the slow lane type.

I wanted to use the pit maneuver, the one often seen on TV, where the cop car slams into the rear corner of the suspect vehicle and sends it spinning out of control. However, because of the oncoming traffic and the gravel shoulder, I didn't think I could perform it safely. I got as close as I could to his car, keeping my options open, and still trying to warn oncoming traffic.

Then for some reason, Mr. Tequila decided it was time to stop. Maybe he had finally seen me behind him and the semi-trucks coming in front of him. But anyway, he stopped in the middle of the fast lane. Not good.

I parked my patrol car centered on the dotted line, between the second and third lane, still trying to warn traffic. I bolted out of the car and around to the passenger side of the suspect vehicle, then I pulled on the door handle. Damn, it's locked. So, I kicked the passenger door window. To my surprise the window just flexed and bowed like a fishing pole reeling in a giant salmon. I tried again with the same result.

By this time another officer had pulled onto the shoulder behind my car. With traffic sufficiently clear in front of me, I ran around to the driver side. This time the door wasn't locked. Out came the driver, by his head: the other officer had arrived just in time to help me drag the suspect into the median and cuff him. The backup officer kept him secure, and I moved the suspect vehicle off of the freeway, then parked my patrol car in front of it.

The driver was drunk and had drugs in the car. He had driven at least four miles, in the wrong direction, on a 70-mph freeway. He was so hammered that he told me he thought he was driving in Wisconsin.

THE FRONT LINES

"Bullshit," I thought.

My training officer had just said, "Every shift is like a tour in Vietnam." He explained what he meant, but I wasn't buying it. This was America. We were not at war, we weren't dropping Agent Orange, dodging sniper fire, or even carrying fully automatic weapons.

However, my career would provide numerous reasons to reconsider the weight of his statement: I personally knew three officers who were murdered while doing their job, three others who were shot, yet survived, and several that had to use fatal force. I don't know how many times I've witnessed life flight crews fly into a scene involving serious injuries, load up the victims and take off again. Like other officers, I've responded to the scenes of traumatic fatal crashes, suicides, gun-shot victims, violent assaults, etc. I was also required to attend a few autopsies. One of which included the body of a child, who was hardly recognizable as human, due to the severity of a multiple vehicle crash.

Like officers do, I've spent many hours on perimeters with an assault rifle in my hands, whether in the rain, in the dark, or during the day, for various felonious situations.

Some occasions called for the rifle. Guys in blue get some strange looks, as people watch them walk through their backyards with an M-4 in their hands.

I think it's fair to say that police officers often see and experience things that are generally only otherwise experienced by front line soldiers during combat.

My mentor told me another thing, which has repeatedly proved to be true, "Sometimes you'll have so much fun that you'd give the department back their money for that day. Sometimes you wouldn't go through that day over again if they paid you ten thousand dollars." This training officer was one of the sharpest men that I would ever have the opportunity to work with.

He had played division one college football at a well-known University before entering the MSP (Michigan State Police), and set an MSP academy record during his time there.

I knew who he was prior to entering the MSP. Every morning, as I went through the academy, I saw his name on the record board above the gym doors. My name never made it onto that board.

The man had an intensity about him that would make the leaves tremble when he walked by. On one occasion I commented to Mr. Intensity, that if I ever had to get into a big pile of shit in this job, I would want him to be there.

We worked through more than a few shitstorms together.

OFFICER DOWN

It didn't take long for me to experience a situation which validated my mentor's war comparison. He wasn't full of

shit, or exaggerating to impress me. At that time, our assigned patrol area covered large rural areas, as well as a rather famous city. The county jail was located downtown,
and we were familiar with the city for several reasons. One
of which was from arresting people from all over the place,
and bringing them through the city to the county jail.

"Shots fired. Officer down." The call came from dispatch
like electricity from a taser. The shooting had happened in a
rough neighborhood of the metropolis. My partner was
driving, and we were about ten or fifteen minutes out.

There are some calls you drive to, some calls you drive fast
to, and some that you push the squad car as hard as it will
go without losing control; this was the latter. I held on to
the "oh shit" handle above the window, and bounced
around as we screamed down the freeway, and onto the city
streets.

"Grab the shotgun!" he exclaimed. I did. That was the first
time I got a long gun ready while responding to a call. It
wouldn't be the last.

We arrived at the scene, in an inner-city neighborhood. It
was just like every other neighborhood in America, at midnight; except the streets were full of people, and gun shell
casings were strewn all around on the ground. For all we
knew the suspects were hiding in the crowd. We met up
with some city officers, got a quick update and began dis-
persing the crowd. The wounded officer had been shot with
an AK-47 during a traffic stop. He was then rushed to the
hospital. No waiting for an ambulance in that type of situation. You throw him in the back seat, one guy tries his best
to attend to the wound, while the driver races to the hospital.

For those who aren't familiar, the AK-47 was the primary
rifle used by the enemy soldiers in Vietnam, and in numerous other wars.

5

One suspect was already dead in the car, as the officers had initially returned fire. But amid the chaos of attending to a wounded officer, trying to keep cover, and return fire, two other suspects got away.

Tips began pouring in. One of the suspects turned up at a hospital well out of the city, seeking treatment for a gunshot wound. He was snagged up after being treated.

Rapid investigation, and following up on tips led to information that the other suspect was inside a nearby house. Officers, including me, had been walking near this house for hours before we found out the suspect might be inside. With shotgun in hand, I took a point on the perimeter, behind a large metal dumpster. My partner was on another perimeter point with the .223 rifle. We stayed there for hours.

As the sun came up, so did the city SWAT team. That's not what they called themselves, but that's what civilians know them as. I watched from my perimeter position after chasing off some media knucklehead, who couldn't put one and one together to figure out that officers hiding behind cover with long guns meant that it wasn't safe to be walking around. I told him what time it was, and sent him packing. Later I saw some video footage on the local news; it was of me looking like an ass as I ran back to cover with shotgun in hand. He got his revenge.

It didn't take long before the SWAT team entered the home. I heard an explosion, the force of which I had not experienced before. The team had tossed a flash-bang into a room. My chest rattled from the shockwave, despite being across the street, and mostly behind the dumpster.

The team did their job well. Nobody got hurt, and the suspect came out in cuffs. His ears are probably still ringing. That suspect had also been shot during the first exchange of gunfire. It was a superficial wound.

The officer who had been shot did survive although he would never fully recover from that injury.

SCHWACK!!!

I arrived on the scene of a domestic violence situation, to back up a deputy who was handling the call. The deputy was interviewing the female involved in the dispute. As I entered the house, I saw a male subject standing in the hallway, maybe twenty feet away from the deputy. As a backup officer, I saw what needed to be done. We had all done this a hundred times. My job was to deal with the other subject involved in the situation.

I contacted the male subject in order to get his side of the story. I asked the man, who was in his late thirties or early forties, to step outside with me and talk. It was more of a statement than a question. He looked me in the eye and said, "After you." At that moment I knew. The look in his eye, and the tone he used clearly indicated that things were headed south. I wasn't about to turn my back to him and he wasn't gonna volunteer to go anywhere.

I asked him if he had any weapons on him and he said "No."

I then asked him if I could check, and he said "Sure." I had him place his hands behind his back during the pat down for weapons. The subject placed his hands behind his back, and interlocked his fingers as requested. I then grabbed hold of his interlocked fingers, and checked him for weapons. Finding nothing, I advised the subject that he was not under arrest, but that I was going to detain him in handcuffs until the investigation was complete. This is a fairly common practice.

"The hell you are. Not in my house." he said as he pulled like hell to get away from me. The finger lock tactic worked and provided me with a few seconds of reaction time. It took him seconds to break my grip then he was moving towards the nearby kitchen. Knives and many other items that can be used as weapons are abundant in kitchens.

7

When a subject is verbally confrontational, disregards an officer's instructions, then attempts to escape, for no apparent reason; you better be prepared in case the SHTF (Shit Hits The Fan). Officers never know who they're dealing with. In this case I also did not know why he chose this course of action. He could have been on parole, had a warrant for his arrest, going for a weapon, or something similar. Police officers are trained to do whatever is necessary to ensure that they go home after their shift.

Those few seconds that it took for the suspect to break my grip bought me enough time to grab him from behind, around the waist. He pulled and tried to break my grip, but he wasn't gonna get out of this without a battle. My options were significantly limited. I certainly wasn't gonna gain control of him while standing and trading punches, or trying to out muscle this guy into a pair of cuffs. When in combat you do what is necessary. Wrestling instincts kicked in and with my arms around his waist, I lifted the suspect off of his feet, and over my shoulder. To the floor we crashed, with him landing first. His head and shoulders smashed a big hole through the drywall in the hallway. You'd think somebody in that situation would give up after that. Nope.

Now on the ground, we were on my turf, where I was most comfortable. He was on his back, on the floor in the hallway. I was perpendicular to him with my chest was weighing on his chest, my left arm trying to secure his right arm and keep him on his back. My legs were spread and I was completely off of the floor, on the tips of my toes, leveraging all of my body weight onto his chest. He was strong; physical labor, brick layer strong. *No Bueno.*

During the struggle, the suspect's left hand was free and he reached aggressively towards me, in the area where no man wants to be hit. Schwack!!! You know, like in comic books where the word is oversized and followed by several exclamation points. I punched him in the face as hard as I could, with my bodyweight behind the strike.

The poh-leece dictionary describes this as a distraction technique, an effort to change a suspect's thought process, usually via physical force. His head bounced off the floor. I hit him hard, but he was still fighting like hell.

Other officers joined the fray. It took several minutes for us to get him cuffed behind his back. The suspect was still not going anywhere voluntarily, and four of us had to carry him out of his house, one officer carrying each of his limbs. Since this was not my case, I don't think I ever found out why he was fighting so hard to get away.

Having been involved in a career full of intense situations, that was the only time I ever had to punch somebody in the face. In fact, it was the only time in my life.

GUNSHOTS IN THE NIGHT

On a quiet night shift, my partner and I were headed down a two-lane highway in a rural area. While he was driving, we heard the distinct sound of several gun shots nearby. This is not something often heard during the night shift. It was not too far from the road we were driving on, in the middle of nowhere. To make matters more interesting there was an unoccupied car parked nearby, on the shoulder of the road, with out-of-state plates.

What would you think? Poachers? Someone shooting at the cops? Homicide(s) in progress? Whatever it was, it was illegal, unusual, and dangerous. We didn't have night vision, nor thermal vision. We had a shotgun and an M4.

We drove down the road, and called out the situation to dispatch. We were headed south, and the shots came from the west side; the passenger side. With headlights out, we turned around and headed back north towards trouble. I had gotten the M4 (.223 rifle) out and walked alongside the passenger side of the patrol car, with the engine block as cover. An extra magazine was stuffed into my back pants pocket.

The shots came from the side of the road nearest my partner. He had the more dangerous task; car doors are not bullet proof, and he wasn't in the best tactical position. The plan was that if shots were fired, my partner would haul ass out of harm's way, in our Dodge Charger, and I would cover him with the thirty rounds in my rifle. I could seek cover behind nearby trees if necessary.

When shit happens sometimes you have to make instant decisions. Looking back, we probably could have come up with something better, but that was the decision we came up with. Backup was headed our way, due to the precarious nature of the unusual circumstance.

Slowly we crept back to the location where the shots had been heard from. Backup arrived, and other officers armed with long guns were out on the highway as well.

Significantly armed and with a halfway decent game plan, we hit the emergency lights on one of the patrol cars, and called out to whoever was out there in the sticks. We employed the effective and all-time favorite police phrase, "Come out with your hands up."

A few young guys came walking out of the wooded area with their hands in the air. They were secured and interrogated. Their story was that they had some new guns and wanted to do some target practice. So, they found a rural area where they thought it was safe to shoot. It sounded like complete BS to me and the other officers as well. We checked the area and found their guns. A K9 team came to assist with the search. Nobody was located. There was no evidence of blood or that anyone had been shot. We seized the guns, searched the car, and identified the young men. Charges were sought for weapons related offenses.

It was unusual to say the least. Who knows what their real motive was? Maybe we had prevented a school shooting.

Maybe they were just stupid kids doing stupid things. Whatever it was, the weapons were no longer in their possession.

MOTORCYCLE MEATHEAD

Troopers from another post area, adjacent to the one where I worked, were pursuing a motorcycle on the freeway. They were headed rapidly in my direction. I met up with a county deputy in the median. We made a plan to attempt to block the fleeing motorcyclist from the front.

As the pursuit neared our location, we pulled out onto the two lane, seventy-mph freeway. The deputy was in one lane and I in the other. We accelerated quickly, as the motorcycle was screaming up behind us.

The two of us increased our speed to triple digits. We were flying, right next to each other in an attempt to block the oncoming motorcycle. The fleeing suspect now had patrol cars behind him and in front of him.

The biker swerved back and forth behind us. He did the motorcycle version of Pavel Datsyuk's NHL juke move. He swerved to the left. Like a goalie that looks like a tool before Datsyuk scores, so did we. The motorcyclist hit the rocket boosters and flew around us to the right, on the shoulder. It was a dangerous move. He squeezed between my patrol car and the delineator reflector poles on the side of the shoulder.

Despite the fact that I was already pushing the patrol car as fast as it would go, the biker blasted past me like I was standing still. These types of bikes are called crotch rockets for a reason. Their acceleration and top speed capabilities far exceed that of even the fastest patrol cars. Our plan to block him turned out to be a futile effort.

The motorcycle screamed into racing speed, and rapidly pulled ahead, until he became a small dot on the freeway in front of us. The bullet bike had blown through our large post area (approximately thirty miles) within minutes. He was just about to enter the next state police post area, where more officers were waiting to continue the chase. After the speedster's tour of Michigan, his bike finally ran out of gas and he pulled over to the shoulder. One of the pursuing deputies slammed his patrol car into park right behind the bike, and tackled the driver off of his speed machine.

The biker was skilled, but he wasn't going out run the radio. Thankfully, he chose to stay on the freeway. A pursuit on the side streets would have been extremely dangerous for the motoring public, and him.

There were several pursuits of motorcyclists, who knew their vehicles were immensely faster and more agile than police cars. They too found out that the police radio is almost impossible to get away from.

On another occasion, I was parked in the median, running radar. Three motorcyclists from a local crotch rocket club crested a slight hill and into the range of my radar. The trio flew past me at speeds well over 100 mph. At that speed it would have been impossible for me to exit the median and catch up with them. Their motorcycle club was well known in our area. They were young guys, who liked fast bikes.

Pursuits are inherently dangerous and I determined that their speeding adventure wasn't worth potential fatalities. That day they got a get out of jail free card. Had they been fleeing from a crime it would have been a different story. Sometimes discretion is the better part of valor.

Chapter Two

CRIMINAL INVESTIGATIONS

ARSON & COLLAPSIBLE BATONS

During a quiet night shift, we cruised through the post area on the lookout for ne'er-do-wells. I spotted an unusual glow in the distance and we headed to check it out. As we neared, it became clear that it was a small fire, on the dashboard of an unoccupied vehicle. We had just missed the firebug and arrived in time to save the car from any major damage.

The car was locked with all the windows rolled up. I had a chance to do my Chuck Norris impression, and whipped out my collapsible baton to bash out the window. The glass didn't shatter, but my baton did. Several pieces of the baton had exploded in every direction.

I asked my partner if I could use hers. She handed it to me. Hers was defective too, and detonated upon impact. The axe in the trunk didn't have any trouble with the window. We blasted the small blaze with a fire extinguisher and saved the fire department a trip.

Sherlock was out of town for the week, so we had to tackle the mystery alone. Our powers of deduction were put to the test, but we finally concluded that the registered owner might be a good suspect. Sherlock would have been impressed.

The subject was an adult female. She was in financial trouble and had arrived at the conclusion that a vehicle inferno would be the best resolution. Surely nobody would be able to solve the mystery once the car had burned to a crisp. Apparently, she wasn't aware that vin numbers are etched into steel in several locations on vehicles, so they can't be burned off.

I told my boss about the poorly constructed batons. He bought us the new and improved model. Then the boss-man officially directed me to discontinue any further use of batons on car windows. I was an obedient trooper and didn't break any more batons. I promptly removed the department issued paperweight from my gun-belt and stored it in a place where it would be safe from car windows.

BEAN COUNTERS & BREAK-INS

Dispatch reported a house break-in, and I was the closest car. So I was off to solve crime, not just take a report. I was trained to have a goal to close out an investigation with the bad guy in jail. This was the duty of a responsible officer.

Somebody behind a desk somewhere keeps track of statistics on what percentage of cases are closed or completed with an arrest, and which are closed as unsolved. These are called clearance rates. The FBI keeps a record of this information, which is available to the public.

Years earlier, my training officer had demonstrated a high motivation to solve the crimes which we were assigned to investigate. On this occasion, I contacted the victim and covered the bases with the information that I could obtain from him. A neighborhood canvas initially seemed a fruitless endeavor to me. However, as I was required to do so, I had come to learn that this was a valuable tool in developing suspects. After contacting a few residents in the area, a local problem teenager (over seventeen / legally an adult), was identified.

He was found at his residence, not terribly far from the victim's home, so I brought him out to the patrol car for an interview. The suspect was not under arrest, and as usual with such situations I advised him that he was free to leave at any time. I often told suspects that even if they confessed, I didn't have to arrest them at that time; that if they complied, I could contact the prosecutor and advise them of their cooperation.

Suspects are very often willing to be questioned. They want to throw an officer off track by covering their trail with a slippery story. They tend to like the idea that they aren't being forced to talk. A helpful tool in encouraging a subject to talk is advising them that a trip to jail is unnecessary that day. It often seemed to ease people into the chilly water of speaking with a police officer.

I flipped over my daily report (a document used for recording times and locations of contacts with people, investigations, etc.), which was attached to a pad of new daily reports, not unlike a pad of legal paper. I was in the driver seat, and he was in the front passenger seat. I asked him to place his left hand on the new daily report. He complied with this simple request.

Then I began to explain to him how easily the police could dust for prints and send them to the forensics lab for analysis. He realized that he had just voluntarily provided me with his fingerprints. Not rocket science I know. He hung his head. Done like dinner.

It didn't take too much longer for him to confess to the whole thing and tell me where the stolen property was. A warrant was sought, he was arrested, case closed. One more checkmark in the desk jockey's spreadsheet.

There's no law against using tricks or even bending the truth (a lot) to get suspects to confess. Countless criminals have been caught with their hand in the cookie jar, simply because they bought the nonsense that officers were selling. Often times there's not enough evidence to arrest a suspect. An interview and confession are frequently where the gathering of evidence begins. With admissions about the location of stolen property, or information only the suspect could know; many arrestees effectively handcuff themselves. But this doesn't happen apart from a motivated officer with at least some interview abilities.

A BELATED
INTRO TO THE MSP

The Michigan State Police is considered a full-service police agency. Uniformed troopers conduct both criminal investigation and traffic patrol. Many agencies have a different model, in which a police officer will take an initial crime report and then turn it over to a detective agency within their department for the investigative portion. This role differs even among state police agencies. In some states, the state police function as a highway patrol only. One is not better than another; there are merely different ways in which police agencies have organized their respective departments.

If an MSP trooper shows up on your door to handle your home break-in case, he or she is responsible for that case from beginning to end, including all of the investigation. Examples of this are highlighted later in this book. We were well trained in latent prints, crime scene photographs, evidence collection, interviews and interrogations, and the other basics of criminal investigation.

There are roughly one thousand uniformed troopers in Michigan, approximately another thousand MSP troopers in non-uniform assignments and civilian employees. These non-uniform assignments include detectives, fugitive teams, narcotics teams, homicide investigation teams, forensic lab specialists, and other various specialty types.

Why detectives, if the road troopers do all their own investigation? Well, detectives in the MSP were assigned to higher profile cases; homicides and other major crimes. In my career I can recall turning only two cases over to post detectives; one was a complicated embezzlement case and the other was merely a motivated detective who stepped up to help. Generally, each post (MSP stations located in different cities/counties) had one assigned detective, but some of the larger posts had two.

MSP troopers work with a partner during the nightshift. The day and afternoon shifts they work single-officer patrol.

PEEK-A-BOO

The 911 dispatcher sent me to another B&E (breaking and entering) of a barn. The victim's home was set back out of view of the road, behind a bunch of trees. There were no houses within view of the residence or barn.

Several tools and a shotgun had been stolen from the older man's barn. It was large building, with a concrete floor. The victim, used it for a workshop as well as storage. I asked him to walk me through the scene, and advise of anything that had been stolen or looked like it had been moved.

I walked carefully around looking for any potential footwear impressions on the dusty floor. There were some, but they were too smudged to be identifiable. The victim showed me some tools that had been moved, then he noticed his large red toolbox had been moved a dozen feet or so away from where it was normally kept.

I looked at it closely; the dust on the top had been smeared around. Near the corner of the toolbox there was a partial footwear impression. It was from the front half of a running shoe or gym shoe. The thief used the tool box to climb onto and access several of the stolen items from where they had been hung. The shoe print was pristine and distinctive. I took numerous digital photographs of it.

Digital cameras were a huge step up from the old film dependent cameras, which I was trained on in the academy. The ancient ones were fairly complex to use proficiently, and I hated them. But anybody can use a simple digital camera, no special photography talent is necessary.

After documenting all of the stolen property, I provided the victim with a business card and report number, standard mostly for insurance purposes. Now it was time to find the thief with the distinctive shoes.

There was a trailer park no more than a few hundred yards from the victim's residence. That seemed like a good place to start looking under stones. I slowly cruised through the trailer park in the daylight. I'm guessing there were maybe fifty trailers there.

I stopped when I saw someone outside and spoke to them briefly. There were a few teenagers hanging outside and enjoying the weather. I checked their shoes patterns, nothing. As my tour of the trailers continued, I observed a lady in her thirties standing outside of her mobile home with a child. I got out to speak with her. The front door of her trailer was open, probably because of the nice weather. While asking her if she knew of any problem people in the area, a young man leaned his head into view inside the trailer, and then quickly back out of view. Bazinga!

I called him out, and was informed that he was seventeen (legally an adult, so no parental permission needed to interview him). I told the young man to sit down on the stairs. He complied. I told him to show me the bottom of his shoes. He hesitated initially but lifted up his foot. From about five feet away I could tell that those were the shoes I was looking for. Cuffs on and seated in the patrol car, he got a free ride to the station.

Interviews and interrogations of seventeen-year olds are usually not difficult. Interrogation is basically just a word for intense interviews; no light bulb swinging from a chord in a dark room with a guy taped to a chair, no waterboarding.

I had obtained a myriad of confessions from adults, without having to break a sweat. An interview can be likened to a battle of wits, and teenagers generally don't stand a chance.

I'm not the best interviewer the department had, but I'm certainly not the worst. My training officer, Mr. Intensity, had the most exceptional interview and interrogation abilities I witnessed during my career. He would get so intense during a suspect interview, that it would make me uncomfortable as I sat there watching him work. He practiced his interview skills on everyone he investigated. On one occasion I watched him break down a man, who reported that someone had hit the back of his trailer while he was parked at a truck stop. My training officer had him sit in the front seat and told me to sit in the backseat, as was his practice during several interviews. I had a front row seat to the whole process. He ground the truck driver's face in his interview blender until the suspect finally confessed to making the false report.

I learned from the best. I wasn't the best. Guys like Mr. Intensity were. But I could hold my own. Obtaining confessions became a personal goal. It was a competition between myself and the suspect, like I know it was with my training officer. If I could get a suspect to confess, I felt like I won. I won't cover the interview train-wrecks that I witnessed, but apparently not everyone gets such solid interview training.

The seventeen-year old thief and I entered the intellectual octagon. I was surprised at his endurance. He had an uncommon and repeated ability to thwart my efforts. But I wasn't leaving without getting him to tap out. I could stay in there for hours if needed. The young man, likely had family that had been in prison, because he would not have put up such resistance otherwise. People who've been to prison know you that don't talk to the cops, and you certainly don't confess your crimes to them.

I brought his shoes in and told him about the evidence he had left at the scene. I confronted him with the idea that he could be held responsible if someone got shot or killed with the gun that he stole. Like an arm bar or a leg lock, I wasn't gonna let go. He finally tapped out, admitting that he broke in to the victim's barn, and stole the gun and tools.

Of all suspects I interviewed, surprisingly one of the most difficult was not even old enough to buy cigarettes.

We wrestled for a while about where the stolen property was, but it didn't take too long to get that information out of him. It was all recovered from behind the skirting at the bottom of the trailer he was staying at.

Now I had a mountain of paperwork to complete for the in-custody arrest. The court required a police report early the next morning for suspects who were in custody. This was policy for all of us. So we stayed and typed until it was done, even if it resulted in overtime, which it often did. Before I had even completed the paperwork on that arrest, the suspect was bonded out by family members. I watched as they greeted him with hugs like he had scored the game-winning touchdown.

If that were me at seventeen: 1) I know my parents would have left me in there until the jail threw me out. 2) Jail would have been the least of my problems. I had been taught to have a healthy respect for authority, the way that most decent people do; corporal punishment.

IT'S LIKE GOING TO CONFESSION

I don't really know what it's like to go to confession, I'm not Catholic. That said, I do know a thing or two about the nature of confessions.

My shift had barely started, and I was sent to the scene of an overdose. A thirty-ish adult male, who had still been living with his parents had been found dead in their home with a heroin needle near his arm. The parents of the deceased had watched him enter the bathroom. They noticed when he didn't come out, then they found him and called 911.

Usually, such an obvious case of a self-induced drug overdose wouldn't get much attention. Why should it? In cases where the victims clearly caused their own death, there is no need to look into the matter any further. This case was as transparent as it could be. Had I documented the basic details of the case in a report, and marked it as closed, it never would have gotten a second thought. No supervisor I ever encountered, would advise a trooper to investigate such a case further.

Normally officers don't lose sleep over drug users who died using illegal drugs. In a few of my cases, my subconscious continued to analyze, and investigate while I slept. But this wasn't one of those cases.

The fact that the parents were so distraught over the matter provided sufficient motivation for me to look into it. They were good people, compassionate people, and they had suffered the loss of a beloved family member.

One conspicuous fact remained. Heroin isn't indigenous to America. Somebody had supplied the illegal substance to the now deceased subject. So, how does one find the suspect(s) who provided the illicit drugs to a dead guy? As my compadre would often say to his assistant, Watson, the answer is elementary. Investigation.

21

One thing is certain, the dealer wasn't going to stroll into the state police post wearing a sign saying he was the guy who had sold heroin to the addict who died from it.

Before video surveillance and camera phones, before GPS tracking devices and remote-controlled drones, there was good old-fashioned verbal communication. By the way don't eat ham and eggs on St. Patrick's Day; strange things happen. Rivers, beer, and chicken ovum turn green. Even Dr. Seuss could have passed Criminal Investigation 101. The thesis of which is that interviews of witnesses are a standard component of investigation. This is not without reason: the wheel of criminal investigation was invented long before the 21st century.

An officer who doesn't carefully and purposefully interview potential witnesses, will not solve many crimes. Officers who don't know how to interview and interrogate witnesses and suspects, handicap themselves as investigators.

Proficiency in nearly any task is generally accomplished by two means: the training and experience of others, and practice. Criminal investigation is no exception to this rule. Every case is an opportunity to develop, and fine-tune investigation aptitude.

The parents of the deceased subject knew his girlfriend. Said girlfriend, knew some of the people that the deceased (and she) occasionally used drugs with. There were several. But a few lived closer than others. Suspects #1 and #2 developed. They were a nice couple, who also lived with their parents. This was a common practice among drug users; apparently, cash is tight when one has such habits.

I located the strung-out lovebirds and interviewed them. The father of one of them tried to intervene. But he was unaware that I did not need his permission. Both suspects were in their twenties.

They were separated and interviewed. Unbeknownst to the duo, I recorded the conversations. Neither subject would initially admit to anything. First things first, get them onto the field. After circling a bit, I walked them into the ball park. Each reluctantly admitted to being involved with heroin. Strike one. They admitted they were friends with the deceased. Strike two.

The pitcher warmed his arm up with the first couple pitches. They weren't being forced to play ball, but voluntarily swung at the pitches anyway.

The knuckleball was tricky. Not many people want to admit they're a heroin user. Even fewer would admit that they sold heroin, let alone that they recently sold heroin to a friend, who died with their heroin in his arm.

Rule number one: separate witnesses and/or suspects. Rule number two: creativity in the interview process is not illegal. Using their words against them, to aid them in admitting to their own involvement was helpful. I spoke to each a few times, alternating between them. They didn't have the opportunity to hear what the other had said. The information, which one may or may not have provided to me, was holding the door open for the other to walk through.

It's like an intersection of sorts. One road is dark and rather unpleasant while the other road is brighter, and more appealing. It's easier for the suspect to confess, if it seems a better route than not confessing. But I was hard pressed to come up with a worse scenario to use as an example. I couldn't tell them, well at least you're not the ones who sold heroin to somebody who died as a result. That may be about as bad as it gets in the whole drug dealing arena.

How would I make this easier for them to admit to? This was the question warming up on my back burner as I was slinging other questions at them. Slowly, we were headed towards the finale. The back burner finally boiled over. I remembered hearing a few stories in the news about some tainted quantity of narcotics which resulted in a string of dead addicts. That was the road I needed to direct them to. After all they weren't the type of nasty people who would want to perpetuate the delivery of a potentially fatal batch of heroin, right? Lives were at stake.

They knocked the dirt of their shoes and took a few practice swings, trying to delay the inevitable. Each of the batters was unable to deal with the unexpected knuckleball. One by one they confessed to delivering the heroin to their deceased friend. It's much easier to say that you really want to save lives, than it is to say you're a heroin dealer who just contributed to a fatality.

"No, trooper, I don't want other people to die."

"Yes, trooper, we were together in the same car when we delivered the heroin to our friend who died."

Strike three, you're out. One right after the other succumbed to the same tricky pitch. Each chose the road that painted them in a better light. They weren't just heroin dealers; they were heroes trying to save their fellow users from potentially fatal drugs.

The case was closed within one shift. I didn't take them to jail that night. I had told them I wouldn't. A few days wouldn't matter anyway. The report and warrant requests were sent to the prosecutor, and felony warrants were authorized. The heroin dealing couple were locked up shortly thereafter.

My insightful training officer would have been proud to see his protégé, following in his footsteps. Yet he had probably never heard about the case. He was plenty busy solving homicides halfway across the state.

PLUNDERWHERE

A woman had called to report that her home had been broken into. I was next up to bat, so I showed up at her front door to investigate. She was distressed, and her underwear drawer had been assaulted. Several pairs had been stolen.

She lived alone, and in a small town. The middle-aged woman also advised me that she had recently received a few perverted phone calls; heavy breathing etc. To say that she was spooked by the situation would be an understatement.

Within a week or two, I responded to another call of exactly the same thing, in the same town. The second middle aged woman had also been getting similar phone calls. Some of this lady's underwear had been stolen, as well as that of her young daughter. A simple thief breaks into homes, a pervert steals a woman's underwear, and a monster steals a child's underwear.

It was open season on monsters. I had bagged a bunch of them during my career, and I wasn't the only one hunting. My co-workers filled their share of tags as well. I had heard the accounts of many. When one of the guys would take down one of the worst people in society, the story would often be told in the squad room. We all appreciated the fact that these swamp creatures had been locked up.

Back to the hunt. I would have told Siri to call the famous detective, but she hadn't been born yet. So, I had to dial the phone myself. Sherlock was a bit perplexed by this case, but suggested a hypothesis; the suspect likely resided in the same town, and phone records might prove helpful. I figured he was on to something. I think it was during that very conversation when he first told me that he was considering some guy named Cumberbatch, to play him in an upcoming film project. Who names their kid Cumberbatch?

A review of the victims' phone records pointed to a land line, at a residence in the same town. (In case you are unfamiliar with the term: a landline is a phone that you cannot take out of the house, or use to play Angry Birds.) I contacted the home owner, an older man, who advised that his twenty-something son also lived there. Suspect developed.

The suspect got to have his turn under the swinging lightbulb. He confessed to making the phone calls to both victims, breaking into their homes, and pilfering underwear at each location.

Two victims, multiple felony charges, and one suspect arrested equaled two more marks in the case closed by arrest column. Due to the unique nature of the case, radio stations in the area played a brief and humorous report about the arrest.

A WOMAN SCORNED

On a wintery night shift, a lady came into the post to report that her live-in-boyfriend was up to no good, of the felony variety. She told us that he had a flash drive with child porn on it, and she had brought it in with her. I'm not sure if any other vile criminal act tops this level of evil and vile depravity. Such miscreants were looked on with intense disdain, even by other criminals.

She gave us the key to her home, permission to enter it, and told us that the suspect would probably be there. A handful of officers joined in on the occasion to lock up the disgusting creature. (That would be a compliment). The suspect awoke to my flashlight and pistol in his face, as well as the other officers who came well-armed to the event. Parasite in custody. He was transported to the interview room, and then the jail cell.

Years earlier, I spoke with a supervisor as to how an officer can go about interviewing such evil people without repeatedly punching them in the face. He provided good advice: think of it as the best way for you to get justice for the victims, and for your strong emotions as well. He advised that the disgusting nature of the incident(s) can be turned into motivation to lock the case up air tight. The advice was solid, but the idea of having to speak to such people face to face, and look them in the eyes turned my stomach.

In addition to the vomitous character of the crime, how does one get somebody to confess to such a thing? Interview training came in very helpful here. It's all about minimizing the crime, and encouraging the suspect to admit to a minimal version, while comparing this to worse crimes generally included in that same category.

Even he was repulsed at the mention of such crimes. Not wanting to admit to anything worse. When I compared them with what he had done, he admitted to his crime almost gladly, in the knowledge that he hadn't confessed to more despicable crimes in that category.

Crime reported, suspect arrested, confession given, all before our shift ended. Despite being nauseated, it was a satisfying feeling that justice had been served. The suspect would be locked up for a significant period of time, and added to the sexual offender registry for life.

UNSOLVED

I recall two unrelated felony cases in which the suspect had been identified, yet each case ended up being closed as unsolved. One was a break-in of a garage and theft of tools. The other was an arson which burned a residence to a pile of ashes. Two marks in the unsolved column.

I put significant effort into the interviews of both suspects who each came into the post to speak with me. This was the ideal situation for an interview. The front seat of a patrol car is uncomfortable, but the small interview room, face to face with a trooper in a sharp blue uniform, is a whole new level of uncomfortable.

Neither suspect would budge. I had no physical evidence, but everything in the case pointed to the fact that they were the perpetrators. I personally had no doubt. Yet a prosecutor will not authorize charges based on suspicion and opinion, evidence is required to make an arrest. Despite all my training and experience with interviews and interrogations, these guys simply would not confess.

I had suspected that one of them might not admit his guilt as he had recently been released from prison. People who spend time in prison are trained by fellow inmates that you never confess anything to the police. He still had his prison muscles at the time, so this lesson was fresh in his mind. This suspect endured round after round in the interview room. He wouldn't tap out no matter how many submission techniques I had in my arsenal. The cage match ended in a draw, but he walked out knowing he had got the best of me. When the interview was over, just before we left the interview room, he said, "You're good."

I thought, "Just not good enough." Trooper Intensity would have had him in tears, and confessing to all the crimes he had ever committed.

The arsonist was guilty, period. Had a jury watched the video of the interviews with him, and his repeated non-confessions, but admission to undeniable coincidences, it would have produced a guilty verdict. He was so obviously the guilty culprit, yet it didn't matter how long I had him in the interview room. It also didn't matter how many intersections I had brought him to, or how easy I made it for him to confess, he wouldn't bite; like a fish that could see the hook sticking out of the worm. Frankly it pissed me off (to quote a fellow trooper's national news making statement).

The suspect was a resident of a state out west. He had flown into a nearby airport and came to stay with family at a residence near the house which was burned down. He owned the house, had bought it for a pittance and insured it as a high dollar residence. To make matters more interesting, I discovered that years prior the house directly next door had been burned to the ground. That house belonged to the father of the suspect.

There was plenty of circumstantial evidence. Some prosecutors may actually have taken that case. Not this prosecutor, not in this county. I made a phone call to the insurance company regarding the house fire. Let's just say they never made an insurance payout on it.

There was an abundance of other cases which ended with the status of unsolved. Many cases simply didn't have enough evidence to follow-up on. The investigations stalled, and so did the cases. While my goal was always to solve cases and get confessions, oftentimes I couldn't even develop a suspect.

HAMMERHEART

If you're paying attention in this field of work, then the longer you spend doing the job, the more tactics you can gather to add to your tool belt. This particular tactic was one I picked up at a training seminar. Our department emphasized continued training. Some commanding officers sent more guys for specialized training than others did, and I've worked for both types.

The guy teaching the drug interdiction class was an out-of-state officer who was extremely successful. His premise was simple. If you are looking at race, you are looking at the wrong thing. *The* indicator is human behavior.

The instructor brought plenty of videos. He and his team were knocking off big loads of narcotics and large quantities of cash, most of which was in hidden compartments. He was big on natural human behaviors as indicators of criminal activity. Most people have some level of increased nervousness when stopped by a police officer. Yet those engaged in serious criminal activity are often noticeably more uncomfortable.

The experienced officer showed videos while commenting on how a suspect's pulsing vein was protruding from his forehead or neck. He would also use a simple tactic of placing his hand on a suspect's chest during a pat down. He indicated that those who are up to no good, big no good, often have their hearts pounding out of their chests. Normal people going to work or to visit grandma, don't have their hearts beating so hard that their pulse is visible in the arteries of their neck.

I used this a few times and had some success. One of those times involved a suspect that I had caught in a B&E, and theft of property. He was facing some solid felony charges and had a criminal record which was gonna make the punishment for these offenses more severe. I encouraged him to try to work off some of his troubles by providing information leading to the arrest of another felon and/or solving other felony crime(s): not just somebody driving on a suspended license, or who always drives home drunk from the bar.

A little leverage on this guy worked. I got the local narcotics team involved as well as a few troopers. Our guy used his cell phone from the jail to contact his cocaine dealer.

Some people order pizza to be delivered to their home, and others order cocaine. The deal was made. The dude in jail gave us a description of the suspect, his car, where and when he was going to meet for the deal.

Everything worked as planned, well almost. Same car, same location, same guy, but no drugs. A drug dog was called to the scene, one from a local department. This particular dog didn't have a five-star reputation.

Nothing.

While talking to the suspect outside of his car, with some backup officers there, I placed my hand on his chest while patting down his pockets again. This guy's heart was about to blow out of his chest.

The car was searched and a set of brass knuckles was found in the center console. In our state this was illegal. So, after searching the car to no end. I transported this guy to the jail for his brass knuckles, and suspected we might find the narcotics there. It was about a thirty-mile trip to the jail. I have never witnessed somebody have such an uncomfortable ride to jail. He was seated in the front seat, cuffed behind his back. Leaning from one side to the other, back to the other, he was miserable, and now I knew where the drugs were.

Upon getting to the jail, I explained the details of the situation to the jail guard/deputy. During a strip search, the guard located the drugs, you know where. The guard advised me that he could see plastic protruding from a place where it shouldn't have been, and directed the suspect to remove it. The suspect complied. He had been sitting on a golf ball size chunk of cocaine, approximately one ounce.

The physical nature and behavior of the human body is often easier to discern than a subject's words. Body language doesn't lie. An experienced officer can tell if a suspect is lying by merely spending a few minutes watching, more than they can by listening.

DINGLEBERRIES

While working an afternoon shift, I was dispatched to handle a domestic assault that had happened at a bar. I contacted the victim, and interviewed her regarding the details. Her drunk boyfriend had hit her, and then driven off in his old blue pickup truck.

It was evening, but still fairly light outside when I started my search for the suspect. His home was maybe ten or fifteen miles from the bar, and his truck wasn't in his driveway. It was in a small neighborhood, not far from a busy four lane road. I drove around the area looking for his truck.

No luck, so I went back out to the main road and headed in the direction of the bar.

By this time the sun had set, and my search just became a little more difficult. When I was nearing the bar again, I observed the suspect vehicle. He was driving in the direction of his house. I activated the lights and siren, but he decided he didn't want to talk to me. It was just another in a string of poor decisions he made that day.

Perhaps he thought the combination of his superior driving skills, and his well-maintained performance driving machine were sufficient to evade a state trooper. I called out the pursuit. It's cliché, I know; you might be able to get away from one officer, but you are probably not going to outrun the police radio. This guy, however, was in no danger of getting away from anyone.

Cops take police pursuits seriously. Generally, every police officer in the area will race to assist the pursuing officer. Police officers will leave a traffic stop or a non-emergency call to assist in the more pressing issue. It is one of the more intense experiences of the job, to initiate a pursuit or to assist in one. Until help arrives, it's just you and the bad guy(s). More often than not, you don't know why the suspect is fleeing. In this case I had the basic idea.

The suspect continued driving in the direction of his house. Once he turned onto the side road leading to his neighborhood, I advised dispatch of the turn and that he was likely headed to his house. Siren blaring and emergency lights flashing, I chased him into his neighborhood, and right into his driveway.

I slammed my patrol car into park, as I watched the overweight suspect exit his vehicle and run. I laughed at the sight. A fifty-year old fat guy has about as much chance getting away in a foot chase, as an old rusty pickup truck has of outrunning a state police car.

I chased him on foot, more jogging than chasing. Foot pursuits usually involve sprinting. Not so in this case. He ran into his backyard and was introduced to my taser. The taser made its loud pop sound as it was triggered, launching the probes towards the target. He dropped to the ground like a deer hit with a twelve-gauge slug.

With the suspect cuffed, I advised dispatch that he was in custody and helped him to his feet. He was walked to the front of my patrol car. Just then a deputy arrived on scene. I searched the suspect more thoroughly in the lights of my car. It was right about that moment when it hit me.

"Sir, did you poop your pants?"

He hung his head. "Yes."

At that point there was no need for him to be fecesious.[1]

In Michigan, state police cars do not have the plastic poo-proof rear seat. The back seat of a state police car is just like the back seat in your car. This was one of maybe two or three cases when I needed to request another agency to transport a subject to jail for me. The deputy on scene obliged.

The sheriff's department did have cages in their cars, as well as the plastic-like poo-proof seats. They also had the helpful jail trustees[2] to do their dirty work; up to and including poo removal.

PHONE A FRIEND

The dispatcher called out the location of a domestic violence situation. I arrived and a back-up officer got there shortly after me. We separated and interviewed the twenty-somethings. I spoke with the attractive female victim.

---

[1] The condition of being full of poop; or having one's colon at maximum capacity

[2] Inmates with non-violent histories who did work around the jail.

She advised that her live-in-boyfriend had a good arm, and excellent aim. He had launched the cordless phone (not an iPhone) in her direction. He was accurate, and the phone had hit her squarely in the side of her face. She had an elongated red 'I-got-hit-mark' on her face. The evidence on her face matched the length and width of the phone.

When I compared notes with the backup officer, we were both rather bewildered to find that the suspect said he didn't do anything. The male subject was placed under arrest. He was puzzled as to why he was in cuffs. I walked him past the victim so he could observe the phone-print on her face.

Had the suspect not had a pitcher's aim, he probably would not have gone to jail. The moral of the story: don't throw phones at friends.

Having lost her boyfriend, the victim was apparently lonely. She left me several messages on my work voicemail, including one asking if I would help her move out. I never returned the calls, but I did find it humorous.

CHRISTMAS CRIMINAL

There's a t-shirt that is seen among dispatchers, and in dispatch centers. It has the phrase, "I tell police officers where to go." Generally, while driving around in the blue car, I went where I wanted to go. It was either to favorite fishing holes for traffic patrol, or for follow-up on some open criminal investigation cases. That is of course, until a dispatcher told me where to go.

A friendly dispatcher sent me to a break-in at an apartment complex. The victim's home had been broken into, and her vast collection of DVDs had been stolen. To make matters worse, it was near the holidays and some of her daughter's presents had been taken as well.

The victim was interviewed. Numerous area residents were questioned as well. Apparently, the victim was sufficiently angered about the crime, that she had been doing her own neighborhood canvas. Between the two of us we were able to come up with some information worth following up on.

A potential suspect, a twenty-something white male was contacted. He was brought to the front of my patrol car. The combination of the uniformed trooper and the angry blue car with the red bubble on top was too much for him to take. Like a potato in a pressure cooker, he got all mushy. He confessed to his involvement in the crime. Many of the DVD's had been pawned off at a used movie/video game business. They were recovered. The repentant suspect went to jail.

A noteworthy fact about this incident is that I had no independent recollection of it. It was only after I stumbled across a thank you letter from the victim while looking through some of my MSP stuff, years after I retired. After reviewing the letter, I did recall the incident. The thank you letter from the victims is attached in the external documents (in the e-book).

THE MAID, WITH THE CANDLESTICK, IN THE LIBRARY?

I responded to a dispatched call of a house break-in. The home owner wasn't present when I arrived, but the maid was. Suspect #1 developed. She got her turn under the bright light. The young housekeeper eventually convinced me that she did not commit the crime. She did, however, admit that she had a boyfriend who had a criminal record and was fighting a drug habit. Suspect #1 scratched of the list. Suspect #2 developed.

The maid, without the candlestick, told me where her boyfriend was staying. I located him and put him in the hot seat. The white male, approximately thirty, had done one thing right. He apparently knew how to land an attractive girlfriend who would put up with his nonsense.

His long criminal history, the new felony charge, and potential prison time sufficed as the bad road. The golden bricked road was full of cooperation, confession, helping to recover the victim's stolen property, and providing information leading to a felony arrest; all in the hope of finding mercy in the hearts of the prosecutor and judge.

He chose the route to the Emerald City. The culprit provided a full confession and the location of the stolen property, and he had some information that led to the arrest of a fellow felon.

I couldn't make deals for the prosecutor. Nary a promise was made. However, I was allowed to make suggestions and inferences, potential though they be.

That a prosecutor might look on a suspect's situation and cooperation in a positive light, usually appears to be a better road than taking the charges straight on the nose. The final decision was entirely up to the prosecutor, despite any officer's conjecture. That said, in my experience, prosecutors did tend to take such factors into consideration.

WAS IT COLONEL MUSTARD?

One of my open cases was a house break-in, involving the theft of a PlayStation. The twenty-something victim had a pretty good idea who the suspect was. The victim practically solved the case for me. He provided a description of the suspect's vehicle, and informed me that he often hid marijuana in the air filter.

On a few different occasions, I attempted to locate the suspect at his apartment. The case remained open for a while, as I was having trouble finding the suspect. Later, while working the night shift, my partner and I were cruising through the apartment complex when I spotted the suspect vehicle parked near his apartment.

We could see that there was a subject inside the driver seat, matching the general description of the break-in suspect. I advised my partner of the situation, and we made contact with the male subject in the vehicle. I could smell a strong odor of fresh marijuana coming from the car.

Since it was a felony case I was investigating, the suspect was known to be dealing weed, and I could smell it; the suspect was quickly escorted out of the vehicle to the concrete parking lot via arm-bar. My partner was a bit surprised to see the level of officer action used in the situation. But where I came from, this would be standard procedure.

The suspect was detained in handcuffs and the vehicle was searched. Needless to say, the break-in victim was right about the weed in the air filter. There was a bunch; it was certainly more than for personal use, about a pound or so.

My partner kept an eye on the arrested suspect, and I contacted the occupant of the apartment. She was cordial, and consented to a search of the apartment. The stolen property was quickly located. The suspect was charged with felony breaking and entering of a residence, possession of stolen property, and possession of marijuana with intent to deliver.

It turned out that it wasn't Colonel Mustard with the lead pipe in the ballroom. It was the thief with the weed in the air filter.

THE NEIGHBOR

A father had brought his young teenage daughter into the post. I was called upon to contact him, and investigate. The complainant, father, explained that his daughter had been sexually involved with one of their neighbors in a local trailer park. The young lady was barely a teenager, if that. Needless to say, the dad was furious. I tried to assure him

37

that I would give the matter my full attention, and that the suspect would be dealt with appropriately.

When I spoke with the victim, she stated that she had been seeing the adult male, aged twenty-five to thirty-ish, who lived not far from her. The young lady admitted that she had been sexually involved with him. She detailed their activities, which did not include intercourse. When asked if there was anything unusual or distinct about the man, she basically explained that he had a ring, which wasn't really a ring, in an area south of his waistline. It was noteworthy information.

The victim, who admitted the contact was consensual, was not old enough to legally give consent. The suspect had no business being involved with a child of this age. He was fortunate that the victim's father, hadn't taken action himself. I think any parent might be tempted to take matters into their own hands in such a situation. I'm glad that he made the right choice, by requesting the police to handle the issue.

After the initial interviews, the father was instructed to take his daughter to the hospital. Some nurses have particular training in gathering any potential evidence in such cases. I received a call from the hospital advising that trace amounts of evidence had been gathered from the victim's person. This evidence was unique to males.

There was sufficient probable cause to arrest the suspect. I requested the assistance of a few officers in conducting the arrest for multiple counts of the felony crime. If a felony is involved, it's protocol to bring additional officers. For some reason, several of my coworkers were happy to join me in the task of locating and arresting the suspect. As you might imagine, such crimes are looked upon with disdain by police officers. We deal with a vast array of criminal activity, and this particular one was of a more despicable nature.

My friends, with long guns, followed me to the suspect's residence. One of the back-up officers was a large man, with a military background. Nobody in their right mind would want to tangle with him. We pounded on the door and the suspect answered. He experienced how fast a person can be placed in handcuffs.

The culprit was brought to the booking area, where he was thoroughly searched. One of the standard questions during the booking process is, "Do you have any piercings on your person." The suspect advised that he did, and then proceeded to remove the non-ring from the appendage in his pants. The item was exactly as the victim had described it, more of a bar, than a ring.

Even if there's already plenty of evidence, there's always room for more. So, we spent some time under the swinging lightbulb, in an uncomfortably small interview room. The suspect confessed, tapping out almost immediately after he had entered the octagon.

Why not be cooperative when the victim had precisely described your special non-ring, and your unique cells had been found upon her person (that's the most discreet way I can explain it). Sure, the prosecutor always appreciates a cooperative suspect, and confessions are an act of good will. He was probably told something like that. It might be a good time for him to show his better side. After all, in his mind he is not a terrible person, just somebody who repeatedly made poor decisions. Almost everybody wants to talk, and paint themselves in a better light, especially when facing felony charges.

Another case opened and closed by an arrest within one shift. One more checkmark in the make your boss happy box. Closing an investigation as soon as possible is ideal. Otherwise, the report would hang in my open case file.

Open cases always required additional investigation, locating and interviewing witnesses, suspects, etc. These cases would often drag on until they were either solved or all reasonable efforts had been exhausted and were closed as unresolved.

Everyone appreciates an open and shut case, locked up tight with an insurmountable quantity of evidence: victims and their families, fellow officers, decent supervisors, and prosecutors. Everyone that is, except the suspect(s) and their defense attorney.

FRIENDLY VICTIMS

While investigating another home break-in, the victims provided information regarding a potential suspect. I located her, and she confessed to the incident, while admitting that she had a bad drug habit. She knew the victims and indicated that she felt bad about the whole thing. I didn't arrest her at that time.

The victims were updated regarding the incident, and I advised them that I would seek felony charges from the prosecutor. Then to my surprise the husband and wife, who had their home broken into, decided not to prosecute.

I attempted to change their minds, but no amount of explanation about addicts and thieves needing to face consequences, could sway them. I also tried to clarify that it occasionally proves to be a turning point in the addict's life. I had known a few people, for whom this was the case.

Instead, the couple chose the forgiveness route. I could understand and appreciate their position. However, experience had taught me that behavior tolerated is behavior perpetuated. There is an old proverb:

"A man of great wrath will pay the penalty,
for if you deliver him, you will only have to do it again."[3]

---

[3] Proverbs 19:19

The same concept is applicable to thieves and addicts. Some might think that going easy on their fellow citizen is the best route. It may actually be the worse of the two options. It is possible to forgive someone for their offense, and still hold them accountable for their actions; they might actually learn from it.

THE CRACK ADDICT & HER MOM

A middle-aged mother had called the dispatch center to report that her adult daughter had been stealing from her. I was in the area so I showed up. The complainant lived in a run-down home, in a nice area. She advised that her live-in daughter had been stealing from her for years. Her daughter had a wicked crack habit that her mother was very aware of.

Tough love was not in the vocabulary of this victim. She had tolerated and perpetuated her adult child's thievery, and her habit. The victim/mother said she had kept her expensive jewelry in her purse, which she kept with her all of the time, to prohibit her daughter from stealing that too.

Apparently, the crack-head daughter had run out of other things to steal. So, when her mom was distracted, she vamoosed with the jewelry. Thousands of dollars of her mother's precious jewelry, had then been traded for what was likely a few hundred dollars-worth of crack.

The thirty something crack-fiend had some paraphernalia relating to her habit in plain sight in her bedroom. She confessed to both her habit as well as her kleptomania and was promptly arrested. For some, a swift confession resulted in some free time prior to a warrant authorization and a later arrest. But this classy broad, she got an immediate trip to the hoosegow.

Parents are undeniably supposed to love their children. They are expected to have the best interests of the child in mind. Generally speaking mothers, especially, are nurturers, but too much nurturing can be a recipe for disaster.

"Maybe he failed Drug Dealer 101..."

Chapter Three

TRAFFIC PATROL

HE'D GIVE YOU
THE SHIRT OFF HIS BACK

We were working a night shift in an inner-city neighborhood. It was an area known for gangs, guns, crime, and chases. During a traffic stop my partner contacted the driver, while I spoke to the passenger. As was typical in this area, not many people carry identification. While you and I might take it everywhere we go, they have reasons not to. Arrest warrants, probation and parole violations were primary causes. Then there were proactive purposes, for instance an attempt to avoid being identified while committing criminal activity. If you get caught, why give the police your name?

Notepads were standard equipment, and this identity-concealing practice was one of the reasons. The notebook in my back pocket, and two pens in my front shirt pocket were used so frequently that it would have torn holes in my uniform: however, MSP uniforms are made of wool, and are nearly bulletproof.

With notepad and pen in hand, I wrote down the passenger's name, date of birth and address. A few questions proved helpful in determining truth from fiction. After given a date of birth, the next question is how old are you. Just like identification, many people don't carry calculators. I'm no mathematician, but I can tell if your date of birth and age don't match up.

In high school I did alright in algebra and geometry. Somehow, somebody convinced me it would be a swell idea to take trigonometry. I guess it may have looked good on a college application? I think it actually might have if you could pass it. The high school I attended had a policy that a student could take one class as pass or fail; no letter grade was documented on your report card, but merely pass or fail. I had never failed a class in school. This is not saying much in light of the standards of our public schools. Anyway, I was drowning in trigonometry. I couldn't even spell it, let alone become proficient in it. I had let the teacher know that I was gonna use my pass/fail option for his class. If ever a student fell upon the mercy of a teacher, it was me in that class. Pity was no doubt the only reason the word 'Pass' appeared on my report card. The teacher had showed me the percentage in his grade book. It would have barely qualified as a D-. He was clearly showing me that he had delivered me from a well-deserved fail.

Anyway you'd be surprised how many people are lacking in even the most basic math ability. Math doesn't get much simpler than calculating age from a date of birth. If two plus two didn't equal four, it equaled handcuffs, at least until a true identity could be ascertained.

The passenger had either passed his math classes, or he was telling the truth. The driver was arrested for something, probably driving without a license. My job while my partner secured the driver was to keep an eye on everybody involved. Once his guy was in cuffs, I was in the clear to get the passenger out and speak to him.

If you've ever wondered why police officers are so often seen doing a pat-down, the reason is safety. Most people will answer no, if you ask them if they have any bazookas or hand grenades in their possession. So also people will generally consent to a search for weapons, even many who actually have a gun on them. I guess they are hoping the consent throws the officer off track, or that he or she will fail to find it.

I asked the passenger to lean on the car during the consent search for weapons. I placed my non-gun side foot between his feet and grabbed ahold of his t-shirt. He was placed off balance as I leaned some bodyweight into the hand that I was holding his shirt with.

At some point in this process the subject decided he needed some exercise. He took off at a full sprint, running right through his t-shirt, which he kindly left torn and in my hand. Maybe I'd keep it as a souvenir. I chased him long enough to realize I wasn't gonna catch him. I got my taser out. As you can imagine, running with a taser in hand makes the red laser aim dot bounce around quite a bit. I wasn't gonna take a chance and probably waste a taser cartridge. Then I'd have some splainin' to do:

Dear sergeant, the reason I used a taser cartridge unsuccessfully was because my aim was poor while I chased the suspect down the street in the middle of the night. Can I have another please?

That seemed like a road worth avoiding.

We searched the vehicle and found a small quantity of cocaine in a baggie on the floorboard of the passenger side. Later on, upon returning to the post, I checked the subject's name and date of birth. There's no way he'd give me his real name before donating his shirt. The info came back to a legit person. A check of the driver's license image confirmed that he did in fact give me his real name and DOB. I got a warrant for his arrest and sent the fugitive team after him. They preferred people with felony warrants.

The suspect may have had a drug habit, but at least he was honest.

NOT LISTENING...

The sun had set for the evening and I was nearing the end of my afternoon shift. The shifts were usually 2-10pm, 3-11pm, 4-12am, or some ten or twelve-hour variation.

I followed a car off the highway and onto a side road, then onto another rarely used side road. The car turned into a truck stop and that's when I activated my patrol car lights. It came to a stop in the middle of a vacant area of the large parking lot. There were three adult male occupants.

It was cold. Michigan is always cold it seems, except for July and August, then it's just mosquitos. Why anybody lives there, I don't know. The state motto is, "Why do I live in Michigan?" Anyway, it was cold; the kind of cold that if southerners visited, they'd need a snow suit, and an Eskimo guide.

I had long-johns under my wool uniform and my ten months out of the year coat. When I broke out the winter coat, I wore it damn near all shift every shift until I put it away in July. Cold really doesn't have much to do with this story, I just remember it was so cold that I thought I ought to tell you about it.

Anyhow, I contacted the driver at his window. He was drunk. So I called for a back-up officer because I had to run this guy through some sobriety tests, and there were two other men in the car keep an eye on. Back up arrived. Sobriety tests failed, the drunk was arrested, cuffed, and secured in my patrol car.

Next, it was time to search the suspect's car. The two passengers were requested to exit the vehicle, and consented to a quick check for weapons. No weapons were found, but it is possible to miss one, so a watchful officer would keep an eye on everybody involved. The back-up officer was standing outside keeping an eye on the passengers while I searched the car. A handgun was found in the car: in Michigan it's illegal to possess a gun while intoxicated. It was the driver's

46

car, driver's gun, he's drunk, so the gun was secured in the trunk of my patrol car.

If there's one gun, chances are higher that there might be another. It's the same if you find some drugs in the car, there might be more. So, I've got the bobble head trooper thing going on, head down search the car, head up look at the subjects, repeat.

Then I saw one of the passengers with his hand plunged deep inside the front of his pants. He said he had to pee. The back-up officer was apparently just chillin'. People hide all sorts of things in their pants: guns, drugs, or the occasional flask of whiskey, etc.

So, I'm out of the car yelling at the guy to take his hand out of his pants. He's not listening. When people don't comply with directions from an officer it is an indication that something is wrong. The volume of my voice increased, as did the intensity, "Get your hand out of your pants." My hand was on my side arm, still secured in the holster.

He's still not listening. The back-up officer, Mr. Mellow is posing for the coolest officer of the month poster. I'm convinced that some officers thought their job was just to stand there and look good.

The lever was pulled, the bay doors were open, and the F-bomb was deployed. "Put your fucking hands up."

"I gotta pee," he said.

I reminded him that he was a grown man and could hold it, and again told him to put his hands up. The dude was still not listening; kind of like Gollum in Lord of the Rings, when he's got his hands over his ears shaking his head, saying, "Not listening." Except this guy didn't have his hands over his ears.

Situation sufficiently escalated. Elevated voice and F-bomb were ineffective. Up the ladder of officer action we go. Who knows what the hell this guy had in his pants? A gun had already been found in the car. I drew my gun from my holster and held it at the low ready, screaming, "Put your fucking hands up!"

The defiant subject finally submitted. He flopped his penis out of his draws, put both hands in the air and started pissing right there in front of everyone. A catastrophe was averted and Mr. Pee-body got a lecture about the serious nature of listening to the instructions of a police officer and why.

The two passengers called somebody for a ride, since neither had a valid license. The drunk guy went to jail, on the way there he kept telling me about how he was gonna beat my ass.

Drunks were always telling officers how they were gonna have our badges or kick our asses, or sue us with their superstar attorneys. If they weren't pissing us off, they were pissing their pants. Who knows how many adults I've watched pee on themselves in the process of sobriety tests?

The first time you watch somebody pee their pants, it's a little shocking. Why is there liquid pouring out of this dude's pant leg...Oh, come on, really? Over time, the bladder control issues transitioned to less surprising, then more humorous, to just plain irritating. It was funny though, as the driver was doing sobrieties, the wet spot in his pants was spreading out, and you're hoping the patrol car camera can catch that detail. The next question is always, "Did you just pee on yourself?" The question was for the video. The drunk guy who admits that he peed himself on camera, while doing sobrieties, is probably not gonna take his case to trial.

After arresting so many, I developed a disdain for dealing with drunks. I think we all did.

SUSPICIOUSNES

A respected trooper and I were working another night-shift together in an inner-city neighborhood. I was driving, and country music was probably playing over the radio. We were just leaving from a traffic stop and began slowly cruising down a side street. A car had come up behind us. It could have passed us before I drove away from the traffic stop, but it didn't. I pulled over to the shoulder and waited. The car behind us waited. Red flags were starting to waive.

The car slowly passed us, and we followed it briefly until it turned into a driveway. I pulled onto the shoulder waiting, watching. The driver exited the vehicle and walked up to the front door of the house. He acted like he knocked a few times and just waited there. The street lights were sufficient to see what was going on. The passenger got out. If nerves were visible, these dudes would have been glowing in the dark. The driver began to walk back towards his car, while the passenger walked to meet him.

That's when I told my partner, let's go talk with them. We exited and calmly greeted the two men on the sidewalk. I recognized the driver as somebody we had previously arrested for CCW (carrying a concealed weapon - a pistol). As I walked up, the passenger quickly put his hand in his pocket and then pulled it back out. He had something in his hand, it wasn't a gun. I asked him what he had, he reluctantly showed me. It was a partially burnt marijuana joint. At the time that was a misdemeanor in Michigan, and you could end up in the county jail. I knew something bigger than this was going on, so I grabbed his wrist.

He frantically pulled, trying to get away, pulling both of us into the road. I took him to the ground. We were wrestling for a bit as I tried to get him cuffed. My partner headed in my direction for help. I told him I got this guy, watch the driver, telling the trooper that we had found a gun on him before. I don't know if the primary reason I remembered him was his unique name, or the fact that my partner and I had previously arrested him with a pistol in his waistband.

It didn't take long for me to secure the guy in cuffs. I was bigger than him, and the ground game was my home turf. During a quick search, subsequent to arrest, for possession of marijuana, I located a plastic baggie in his pocket, full of heroin. For some reason the heroin was wrapped in a bunch of individually folded portions of lottery tickets. I wasn't the only one to find heroin packaged in this manner.

The passenger was a smaller guy, shorter than me and didn't have an ounce of fat on him. We knew how the game was played. He was the designated runner. In the bright lights of the jail he looked like a track champ. Dealers would have runners that had the assigned job of outrunning the cops, if needed. There is no doubt in my mind that if I hadn't grabbed his wrist when I did, he would have been off like a rabbit and neither my partner nor I would have had a chance at catching him.

Felony possession of heroin, with intent to deliver. It was a hefty charge, but it wouldn't be long before he'd be back on the streets again. The criminal justice system is so often a revolving door. A guy gets locked up for a while, released, and then locked up again. Some guys had criminal history records as long as I am tall or longer.

Catch and release, repeat as necessary.

SPEECHLESS

Window tint is illegal in Michigan. A Suburban with blacked out windows passed me as I was parked in the median of the freeway. It was a bright sunny afternoon, and I stopped the vehicle for the traffic violation. It was referred to as a fix-it ticket. This means that if you fixed the problem and showed any police officer in Michigan, they could sign off on the ticket and you mail it into the court with no fine.

With dark window tint on a vehicle, an officer never knows what to expect. The occupants aren't visible; it's the traffic stop equivalent of searching for someone in a dark room. I approached the vehicle on the passenger side. This was my preferred approach as I would rather be as far away from traffic as possible.

As I neared the front passenger side window, it began to roll down. Seated in the passenger seat, was one of the most beautiful women I have ever seen. I was literally speechless. Usually I had my standard phrase prepared for the driver/occupants; greeting, identifying myself as a trooper, and advising of the reason for the traffic stop. I had said that phrase so many times that it was muscle memory. There I stood, in shock, unable to get any words out of my mouth.

It must have been several seconds. It was certainly long enough to make it awkward for all of us. Maybe it wouldn't have been so shocking if there were no window tint. Yet this lady was so stunning that even if she hadn't been hidden behind window tint, I might have had the same reaction.

I finally caught my breath and managed to convey the above information. I obtained the driver's license and registration. He was obviously a professional athlete, he had on a Under Armor type shirt, and looked like Terrell Owens during pregame warm ups. During a brief conversation with the two occupants, he informed me that he played football for the Chicago Bears.

It made sense that such an arresting, attractive woman would be hanging out with him. I returned to my vehicle and kept shaking my head. It was like I had been punched in the face and was trying to gather my senses. The experience left me dazed for a while.

After the traffic stop, I called my friend at the dispatch center, and asking him to check the name of the driver on Google. I wanted to see if he did play for the Bears. Sure enough, he did. I hadn't recognized his name. He wasn't one of the more famous players on the team.

At that point I decided that I needed to grow about seven inches taller, and workout all day every day, and exchange my genes for that of a track star. Nah, even then I wouldn't have had a chance. There are some things that are just plain impossible.

James Bond would have been impressed.

GINORMOUS

During my career I encountered one other NFL player. This one was during an afternoon shift. The sun had set for the evening, and I was gonna write a few more biscuits before my shift ended.

Another traffic stop, and I approached on the SUV on the passenger side. The dude driving the vehicle was a descendant of Goliath. I obtained the necessary documentation. I asked where he was headed to; a standard question.

The driver advised that he was headed to Wisconsin. He said that he played football there. I said: "Oh, you play for the Badgers."

He laughed, and said, "No, the Packers." I looked at his license and read his name. I felt like a tool. I told him that if I would have read his name, before asking the question, I would have known who he was. He was a prominent figure among the ranks of NFL defensive lineman. Anybody who knew anything about football, would have known who this guy was. I remember his name, but you can play some trivia.

I had worked with several guys who had been college football players, a few of them had battled in the trenches. The biggest, most formidable of them was probably the biggest human being ever to wear MSP Blue. He was the guy who brought a gallon of water to work with him, every day. I brought a twenty-ounce bottle.

This NFL lineman, made my giant MSP friend look like a child. His hands were the biggest hands I have ever seen. I'm guessing he had some custom work done on his ride. Standard seats, even in the biggest of vehicles, don't go back that far.

We spoke for a few minutes on the shoulder of the freeway. He didn't get my autograph, and I didn't want to bother him by asking for his. I figured he did that plenty enough already. The thought occurred to me to shake his hand, but I don't like hospitals.

Meeting him gave me a whole new appreciation for the NFL running backs. Who would want to play a game that involved being tackled by guys like him? Maybe that's why they get paid so much money. No fool would do that for my salary.

QUEEN FOR A DAY

During a traffic stop on the freeway, the driver was found to have a warrant for her arrest. The lady was wearing a dress and was rather congenial. I secured her in cuffs. There were two additional occupants in the car, and they told me they were headed back from a gay ball. I was a bit perplexed at the idea, but whatever floats your boat, I guess. During a search of the vehicle, I located something so disconcerting that it is forever lodged in my memory.

It was a trophy, which I was told had been won at the gay ball. It wasn't the trophy that was troubling, it was the words etched into the small metal plate at the base. It said, "Queen of the damned, mother of all mothers, who wants hell on earth." I don't recall any other trophy inscriptions encountered during my career. Yet for some reason that one seemed more than just odd.

As if that wasn't sufficient to fill my strange experience quota for the day, I was in for another surprise. The lady was booked into the jail for the arrest warrant. A few minutes after the guards took her to her cell, they returned to advise me that she wasn't a she after all. This was rather unexpected. The subject had the physiological upper torso of a woman, but apparently also the lower half of a male.

I pondered the incident for a while. My musings resulted in a question which is more rhetorical than anything: was there a correlation between the strange inscription, the gay ball, and the lady who turned out to be a man?

HE WON'T NOTICE

Observation of behavior lead me to many arrests. Sitting in the median of the highway only allows for a few seconds of evaluation. Human nature and behavior can often be strong indicators that something is wrong.

The male driver gave me the 'Oh shit!' look as he passed by. Once you've watched ten thousand cars drive by, it becomes easier to notice when something is awry. His physical response to my presence in the median was rather conspicuous. So, I drove out of the median and followed him. What do you know, he took the very first exit available.

I followed him onto the exit ramp and watched as he opened his door, while driving, and dropped a brown paper bag on the road. So, I stopped for a moment and picked up his package, without getting out of my car. Perhaps I should bring it back to him and remind him not to litter.

Marijuana has an unmistakable odor. My nose told me what was in the bag the moment I picked it up. I'm guessing it was a half-pound or so. I stopped him for some traffic violation, and the littering issue.

The white male college student, apparently sold drugs as a side gig. In his car he also had dozens of t-shirts with marijuana logos on them. I've seen one of them a few times. It was a brown shirt, with what appeared to be a UPS logo, and the phrase, "united pot smokers."

During an interview, the subject explained that before college he was on the straight and narrow. He had come from a family that was drug free and did not have the criminal legacy that others do. The turning point came when he met his weed slinging roommate. The suspect started making some cash, and voila, he got to meet me. He also got to meet the jail guards and a prosecutor, as he faced a felony drug charge. He must have failed drug dealer 101. Maybe he dropped that class, like he did his weed.

SUBCONSCIOUS PHYSICAL REACTION TO EXTERNAL STIMULI

Nice weather was good for two things in law enforcement; traffic work, and inner-city violence. My patrol car was parked in the median, tucked in tight behind a cement barrier. Motorists had little time to see me and react to the presence of the eye-catching blue car. It was a great fishing hole for speedy fish.

A vehicle passed me in the fast lane. I noticed one headlight out in the red vehicle. What was more prominent was the driver's physical reaction to my presence. So I pulled out of the median and headed in the direction of the rolling defective equipment violation, with the nervous driver.

The one-eyed car took the first exit available, and then the first turn available. That's when I initiated the traffic stop. The little intuitive guy on my shoulder was screaming at me at this point. Upon contact with the two occupants, they were noticeably uncomfortable.

I knew one of the K9 teams was working only a few miles away. I called the officer and requested his assistance. Police dogs are legally allowed to walk around the exterior of a vehicle for no reason at all. The occupants of the car had no expectation of privacy in the air around the vehicle. The dog did his work and gave a clear indication that the little fella on my shoulder wasn't pulling my leg.

The K9 handler confirmed his dog's positive alert signal. That alone amounts to a legal reason to search the car. Stashed under the back seat was one of the largest quantities of cocaine I had ever seized; two kilos. There were only a few others in my entire career. The estimated value of the anxious driver's cocaine was approximately forty to fifty thousand dollars.

On another occasion, during an unrelated traffic stop, I netted the same amount of cocaine. This time it was stashed really well... in his backpack, on the backseat. Both of those incidents were what we called cold traffic stops. In other words, there was no prior information leading to the stop and subsequent arrests.

Even a blind squirrel finds a nut every once in a while.

REASONABLE SEARCH

A motorist was driving on the freeway, heading to Wisconsin, which unbeknownst to him was also in my direction. I stopped the vehicle for some traffic violation. Upon contact with the driver I immediately noticed a strong smell of fresh (unburned) marijuana. For those of you who are unfamiliar, there is a distinct difference between the smell of fresh or burned. The strength of the odor of fresh weed was indicative of a significant quantity.

I asked the driver about the smell of marijuana in the car. He gave some excuse, and refused my request for consent to search his car. Not that I needed it. When a trained officer notices the odor of marijuana coming from a vehicle that equals sufficient probable cause to search their ride. In the academy were literally trained to recognize the odor of marijuana. An instructor burned some marijuana in a classroom so those of us who have never been around it could become familiar with the smell. I didn't need his consent, but asked for it nonetheless. This guy was one of the few people who ever refused to give me consent to search.

It was within his constitutional right to refuse to give consent to search. He was protected from unreasonable search and seizure (Fourth Amendment). That said, the search would not be unreasonable in light of the strong odor of marijuana.

Being my congenial self, I continued to converse with him. Finally, he admitted that the marijuana I was smelling was coming from a burnt marijuana roach in his ashtray. The driver then proceeded to show me the item.

He was kind enough to help build my case. Possession of even a small amount of marijuana, burnt though it may be, was an illegal and arrest-worthy offense, in Michigan. The driver was placed under arrest, and secured in handcuffs.

I searched the vehicle and located approximately six pounds of marijuana in the trunk. The misdemeanor charge of possession of marijuana just got upgraded to a felony charge of possession with intent to deliver. It was certainly more than for personal use. But maybe he smoked a lot of weed? I don't know, I don't smoke weed, and never have; not even like a former U.S. President, who didn't inhale.

THE FEDS

A federal agency had done their homework on a narcotics case. They were following the suspect vehicle, and called our dispatch center requesting a patrol car to stop the suspect. I was in the area and stopped the vehicle for a traffic violation. A K9 team was called to the scene, and positively indicated on something in the vehicle.

The only item located in the trunk was a large box of laundry detergent. Upon closer inspection, it appeared that the top seal had been finagled with, and resealed. The suspicious box was searched and found to contain three bricks of

cocaine, buried in the laundry detergent. It had an estimated value of sixty to seventy-five thousand dollars.

Federal crimes generally result in more prison time. That
said, I wasn't originally taught that state police, or local
agencies can take a case into the federal system. If so, a federal agent would have to become the charging officer.
Maybe I didn't watch enough *Law and Order*.

The difference between a case getting charged federally or
not, is usually a matter of a phone call. The case must meet
certain criteria, like a particular quantity of narcotics, or a
combination of situations. Later in my career, I knew a few
DEA and FBI agents by first name, and had their cell phone
numbers. By then, I had an idea which cases could be
charged federally. If I wasn't sure I could just pick up the
phone.

Not once did I see a pissing match between federal, state,
or local officers. It makes for good TV, but in reality, at least
in my experience, nobody pushed anyone around about jurisdiction there's plenty of work to go around. To take a case
federally it generally meant that the suspect was going to
face a more significant prison sentence than it would be
with state charges.

In regards to this particular traffic stop, the feds just
wanted the situation to look like it was random. They didn't
want to tip their hand, and no doubt had good reasons and
potentially more suspects involved in their investigations.

THE ROAD RUNNER

I was hiding behind another large concrete bridge support
and lighting up ruthless speeders. The radar units had an
audio tone that was designed to correspond with the digital
display of the vehicle speed. After using radar for so long,
the speed of the vehicle could be estimated by an officer
merely by the audible tone.

Part of the training to use radar involved the visual estimation of the speed of oncoming vehicles. Years of traffic
enforcement turned an officer into a virtual radar unit. The
three elements were used to confirm speed; the officer's visual estimation, the digital display, and audible tone.

As I sat there waiting for the next autograph winner, I saw
a black blur fly past me. The radar unit screamed a high-fre-
quency tone, the digital display read 126 mph. There was no
way I was able to visually estimate the speed of this one, I
didn't have enough time. That was the fastest speed I had
ever clocked on radar.

Sometimes it takes a minute or two to safely pull out of
the median. Then it takes a bit of time to go from zero to a
speed at which you can catch up with the subject. In this
case I didn't have a chance. I called out on the radio with my
less than detailed description of a black sedan traveling at
126 mph eastbound on the freeway. Usually a description
should be more like; a black four door Ford Taurus with
tinted windows and stickers on the rear windshield.

I never caught that one. I did, however, write a handful of
triple digit speeders during my career. Their insurance companies probably appreciated it, their premiums not so
much.

"Curiosity caught the culprit..."

Chapter Four

COLLABORATION

THREE TROOPERS, A FEW FELONIES, & A CASE SOLVED IN ONE SHIFT

I was the nearest officer to the scene of a B&E. I arrived to find a family member at the scene. The elderly home owner had recently passed away, and the home had been broken into: the car was stolen, as well as some personal property, collectors' coins and the like.

Three of us were working during that particular day shift. One of my buddies showed up to help me; dusting for fingerprints, taking photographs, etc. I advised him of the stolen property, and the vehicle was reported to dispatch as stolen. The trooper then contacted some local pawn shops looking for the stolen property.

I spoke with family members of the deceased victim. One of the family members had a criminal history and was therefore a potential suspect.

I contacted some neighbors in the area. When I got to one of the houses directly next door to the victim's residence, I encountered a teenage neighbor and interviewed him. While speaking with him, he advised me that his family member, a cousin in his early twenties, had recently moved in with his family because he had gotten into trouble at home. It was clear that this was the guy we needed to find.

Meanwhile my buddy who was trying to track down the stolen property found it at a local pawn shop. The knuckle-head who sold it had to show his identification in order to do so. The coins were uniquely identifiable. Suspect #2 identified.

We shared this info with the third trooper, who had been working on another case. That trooper was familiar with the second suspect, and knew where he hung out. All three of us went to an apartment complex across town and after a bit of checking around we located both suspects in one of the apartments. Suspect #1 had some of the stolen property in his pants pocket.

The third trooper took one suspect into his car and I took the other. Now it was an unspoken race to see who could get their suspect to confess where the stolen car was first. Between the two of us we quickly gathered information from both suspects and found the car on a seldomly used dirt road about a mile from the apartment.

The family of the victim was contacted, the stolen property was returned, including the stolen vehicle, and the suspects were hauled to the county jail. The family was very grateful, and impressed that all of this could be accomplished in one day.

A BUNCH OF CONDOMS & SUSPECTS

A young lady ended up in the hospital as the result of a sexual assault. I responded there to take her report. At the hospital she showed me some of the bruises she had on her legs and told me the story. Right away I requested a female officer to come and take photos of her injuries. This was the prudent thing to do considering the location of some of her bruising.

The twenty-something victim had chosen to go to a party that involved some of her friends, drugs, alcohol, and a bunch of people she didn't know. Things got out of control when she ended up alone in a room with several men. Inebriated though she was, she didn't deserve what happened next.

The victim was raped repeatedly and passed out. She later awoke alone in the room with about a dozen used condoms laying on the floor all around. As she was providing the information to me, she indicated that she remembered several of the suspects' faces, but only knew one of them by a nickname.

A search warrant was obtained. Several officers assisted me with the search of the residence and the gathering of evidence. There was a lot. While we were there with several patrol cars in the driveway, Mr. Nickname showed up. No doubt he still regrets the decision not to drive on by. Who knows, maybe if he hadn't shown up, he might not have been identified. Curiosity caught the culprit. Suspect #1 arrested.

He took a number and was called into the front passenger seat of my patrol car which doubled as an impromptu interview room. Mr. Nickname confessed to details that were incriminating enough to arrest him. The victim would later confirm that he was in fact one of the men that had raped her.

One of the other suspects was bright enough to show up at his buddy's court hearing (Mr. Nickname). The victim, who was visibly shaken, got my attention. She pointed out the subject to me, and said that he too, was one of the men that had raped her. He was placed in handcuffs immediately, and brought to the jail. Suspect #2 arrested and also confessed to the crime.

A third suspect was ultimately arrested due to the excellent work of a responsible dispatcher. He had heard about the incident and days later put together information gained from a phone call to the dispatch center. He sent another trooper to deal with it immediately. The seasoned trooper who responded, did his job well, and obtained a full confession from suspect #3, who was promptly arrested. The civilian dispatcher did more than was expected of him, and played an essential role in the arrest. Had the dispatcher not acted, the third suspect might never have been identified or arrested.

DNA evidence obtained at the scene sealed up each of these three cases. There were four DNA profiles, but I presume after the three amigos were locked up rather quickly, the other suspect made a run for the border.

THE CHEESY PHOTO

The victims lived in an extremely rural area where large farms and wooded acres were their only neighbors. They had not one, but two of their vehicles stolen from their driveway during the night. The middle-aged married couple always left their keys in the car. Why not, when you live in the middle of nowhere?

I documented the relevant information. There were no neighbors in the area to contact. At that point there wasn't much to proceed with, aside from having dispatch enter the stolen vehicles into LEIN/NCIC (Law Enforcement Information Network/National Crime Information Center). If any police officer located and checked the vehicles license plates, they would be notified that the cars were stolen.

Later during the same shift, dispatch advised me that a city officer had located one of the vehicles, abandoned in a wooded area. I contacted the officer where he found the car. I had known him on a first name basis for years. Inside the vehicle was a paper photocopy of an image. The picture was of an adult male and a child. It was the type that people would take in a photo booth, and the humorous thing about the image was that it included a Chuck E. Cheeses banner.

There was only one of those businesses within at least fifty miles. Neither the first officer nor I could identify the subject in the photo. I presumed it didn't belong to the victims. Before I headed off to get some pizza and ask some questions about the photo, I wanted to check with another city officer.

The other officer at the local police station reviewed the image, and advised that the subject looked very familiar. We did some more checking at the station and identified the suspect.

The vehicle was returned to the victims: they confirmed that they were not familiar with the subject in the photo. I couldn't locate the suspect, that is until I discovered that he and his buddy had been arrested for some other criminal mischief escapade. The cheesy suspect was interviewed at the jail. He confessed to the matter, and said that it was his son in the picture with him. He also told me who his compadre was in the thieving of the vehicles.

Suspect #2 was also interviewed, and confessed to his involvement in the incident. Both of them were charged with felony vehicle theft.

Chuck E. Cheese's was added to the list of locations to check when investigating stolen vehicle cases.

FOR SALE BY OWNER

I arrived on the scene of a dispatched call of a vehicle theft. The victims were a middle-aged couple, who had been in the process of trying to sell their vehicle. A man and woman answered an online ad for the car, and arranged to purchase it. The male subject wrote a check and they departed with the car. However, the check proved to be no good.

The victims had thought it strange that the guy who wrote the check did so while wearing leather gloves. They didn't listen to the little people on their shoulders telling them that something was wrong. Instead they opted to trust complete strangers. Average law-abiding citizens are often naive, and tend to default to trust. Victims are frequently caught off guard because of this. Most people haven't had reason to default to distrust. An attentive citizen, who is mindful of the state of our society, via the news and many other sources, might arrive at this conclusion. However, many do not pay attention, and are dangerously naive.

Aside from the victim interviews and obtaining the check as evidence, there wasn't really anything else I could personally do with the investigation. There are numerous auto theft teams throughout the state. A guy who was assigned to one of those teams, was a friend of mine, and he continued the investigation with the tools he had available.

My buddy did his job well, as he always did. He located the vehicle a few states away. The suspects involved were part of a large auto theft ring. Within a few weeks of making the report of the incident, the victims had their car back. They were pleased with the work of the MSP. Team work solved another case.

End of shift discussions, while sitting in the squad room, often resulted in cases closed with arrests. One officer would say, I know that guy and where he lives. Another would say that sounds like the case I had, the guy is locked up if you want to interview him. This also happened during contact with officers from other agencies. They dealt with the same people and the same crimes. Simple conversations between officers resulted in numerous arrests.

MSP K9 HANDLERS

From the first time I witnessed a demonstration of the abilities of a highly trained police K9, I was impressed.

These brilliant animals would continue to amaze me throughout my career. The MSP used German Shepherds exclusively. This breed is so adaptable, that they can be trained for a multitude of tasks. We had dogs that were most often cross-trained for two different purposes, like tracking and narcotic detection. We had dogs who were trained to detect explosives. We also had cadaver dogs; I got to see one of those specially trained Shepherds in action, only once in my career.

The MSP dog handlers were chosen through an intense selection process that involved interviews, traversing a lengthy obstacle course for time, excellent physical fitness and more. Our department had the opportunity to pick from among the best troopers for this position. For example, one of the MSP K9 handlers I knew was a former Army Ranger.

I saw some excellent K9 teams with several local departments. But as a rule, the MSP dogs and handlers spent a lot more time training, and this showed in their results. They had one training day every week or two and some longer training events throughout the year. I don't think the local departments could afford to keep up with such a rigorous training program. Many agencies had dogs that were solid when it came to narcotics detection, our dogs did that as well, but they were known for their excellent tracking abilities.

MSP policy was that if a dog handler was on a track, somebody went with him as a back-up officer. That meant a guy in a sharp blue uniform would try to keep up with the powerful German Shepherd pulling his handler towards the bad guy. If they went through the brambles and muck, so did we. If they climbed sand dunes in the pouring rain, so did we. Amazingly the dogs often found the suspects, even after tracking for several miles.

NO 'I' IN TEAM

Hundreds of thousands of dedicated police officers across this great country have myriads of their own stories. Many of the people I have had the opportunity to work with have shared the accounts of some of their experiences. While I did not witness these events firsthand, I know these officers, whose word is as reliable as video evidence.

Some of their stories involve physical combat, gun battles, and adrenaline pumping pursuits. They include criminal investigations which landed untold numbers of people in prison, for various felonies. From foot chases to physical altercations, from combat to chest compressions; my companions and coworkers all have war stories. Working together was a welcome necessity.

Whether as backup, helping at emergency calls for service, serving search warrants, conducting investigations, and more, teamwork is an essential aspect of law enforcement.

"At least he didn't have to use a giant inflatable ducky."

Chapter Five

MICHIGAN STATE
POLICE ACADEMY

BOXING PROGRAM

I was told before the academy that the goal of the boxing program was to have you step into the ring with someone who was your physical superior, someone who would put a whoopin' on you, who could introduce you to what it felt like to be hit really hard. After the boxing program was complete, I agreed; that seemed to be the exact point. They certainly weren't teaching boxing, they didn't have the time, nor any expert there to teach relevant skills.

The instructors were repeatedly beating the same message into our heads: never give up. We were gonna have an opportunity to put that into practice. Each recruit would have a minimum of three different opponents. There were a few women in our recruit school. They got to box each other, then each had to step in the ring with a male recruit; who was assigned to hand deliver the gift of seeing stars. There was a punching bag in the room to warm up with, for those who were next up in the ring. We were equipped with red headgear and red gloves with which to pummel each other.

I had a punching bag in the basement from the time I was about 12. My dad was always interested in martial arts, so we dabbled in them here and there. I learned the basics;

how to punch without damaging your wrist, how to using boxing wraps, and some basic technique. Other than that, my instructor was the bag. I'd wrap my wrists and use bag gloves (leather gloves without padding). It was a water bag. It hung heavy, filled with water in a center tube and wrapped in layers of what looked like carpet padding, and covered with a tough leather exterior.

Punching bags are listed on the top ten ways to help teens deal with their frustrations. At least it was in my house. That very bag is presently sitting on my front porch empty of water, just waiting to be hung up and beat on again. This time it will be my offspring pounding on it. They'll have the same teacher as I did; the big bag which would take everything you could throw at it.

Bruce Lee's famous book, *The Tao of Jeet Kune Do*, had been in our home since I was a kid. My dad was a huge fan of his, so I was too. We watched Bruce Lee movies more often than most people would think was prudent. My dad was no Bruce Lee, and neither am I. But we had learned some basic principles from that book that would prove to be helpful on occasion. Boxing in the academy was one of those.

The first few boxing matches seemed to be primarily for instructor evaluation, in order that they could finally match you up with someone who was gonna clobber you. My first two matches went about the way I thought they would. I felt really comfortable throwing punches, and keeping my guard up. I think I got the best of the first two guys; though they may have been draws. Either way, those guys were not designated bell ringers. Out of the ring, my bell had yet to be rung. I was feeling fairly confident.

Unfortunately, some poor schmoh had to draw the short straw of teaching one of the ladies what it was like to get hit by a man. It was a lesson they needed to learn. They needed to have a healthy regard for A) what it felt like B) why they wanted to avoid this. No guy wanted to step in the ring with one of the ladies. I certainly didn't, but I drew the short straw.

Into the ring we went. My corner instructor gave me directions which basically amounted to go easy on her at first and then hit her like you mean business. I felt bad, really bad. The poor girl who stepped into the ring with me was maybe 120 pounds. I was 170 pounds. During several of our long-distance runs, she'd be right there next to me. She could out distance run me all day, every day. We occasionally ran next to each other and I had grown to respect her gumption.

We circled around in the ring a bit, I let her hit me, like I was told, then the green light from my corner. Wham! I hit her hard with a straight right hand. She went down, just like you would imagine any 120-pound female would do when hit by a guy fifty pounds heavier than she. I hoped the lesson was over, I didn't want to do that again. They got her up and let her get her sea legs and told her to head back for more.

No doubt this was a gut check for her. Was she gonna keep going, or was she gonna give up? I knew she had a tough spirit, and I knew that she would step back in as soon as she was able to see straight. She wasn't the type to throw in the towel. Now, I felt even worse. Second verse same as the first. Another stiff right hand to the noggin, and down she went. They would have been cruel to make her do it again.

My turn. I was paired up with a former Marine ____ (not saying). He was about a decade older than me, and somewhere between 215-230 pounds of mean and angry. It was literally my goal in morning P.T. to keep up with him. Our morning physical training sessions varied significantly, and my target was always on him. I thought I had better be able to get my ass in gear enough to keep up with him. He wasn't old, but his age and combat experience motivated me. I worked like hell to keep up with him.

Once I found out my next match was with him, I went into psych myself up for serious competition mode. As a former wrestler, I knew who the bad dudes were, and I had learned the skill of mentally preparing myself for a real contender. My freshman year, I wrestled the same guy, a senior from a nearby school, four times. The dude looked like he had been sculpted out of marble, and he was from a wrestling family. Needless to say, he beat my ass all four times. There were a lot of ass-whoopins' handed out on school wrestling mats.

I went to the warm up bag. As I was pounding on that bag, I was trying to mentally prepare for the looming battle. The song, *'The Eye of the Tiger'* was replaying through my mind, literally. Why that song? I don't know. It wasn't a favorite song and I didn't have the album. I just think my subconscious knew I was about to step in the ring with the guy who had been handpicked to kick my ass. I've often wondered if the instructors paired me up with this dude because I had hit the girl too hard, twice. Either way, their goal was for me get a beatdown.

We entered the ring and he hit me harder than I've ever been hit. We traded punches. I thought, "If he keeps hitting me like this, I'm gonna go down." Instinct kicked in and six years of wrestling experience took over. Double leg takedown. I took him to the ground. Just so you know, you're not supposed to do that in a boxing match. The large MSP referee picked us both up by our headgear. He said something like, "This isn't a bar brawl, I want to see some punches thrown."

The takedown had bought me enough time to shoo the little blue birdies away from my head. Don't let him hit you. Keep your hands up. Send some bombs in his direction. My mind was spinning; do something quick knucklehead, or you're about to get handed a couple minutes of staring at the ceiling.

Another gear was needed. I shifted into four-wheel drive. This guy was gonna get everything I had and more. It wasn't about looking good or bad in front of instructors or buddies. This was about combat, pure and simple. Like so many wrestling matches were: two guys stepped on the mat, and gave their all. At the end one guy gets his hand raised. The break from the takedown was for me like a break between periods during a wrestling match. It was during those times you had a moment to strategize and dig down deep inside your heart for more motivation.

Each of us left our corner. During the battle he landed a solid blow that sent me to the mat. I caught him with a hard right, and he went down. I recall him getting up from the mat at least once, not including the wrestling takedown. We both exited the ring knowing that a battle had taken place.

Many years afterwards the two of us had the rare opportunity to work on an assignment together. A respected supervisor was working with us. We had some time to talk while working in the summer sunshine. I asked the former soldier to tell the boss about the time we stepped into the ring. He did. He recalled the skirmish and had some interesting things to say, but I'll leave that to your imagination.

MY INTRO TO THE MSP

Prior to becoming a trooper, I had never considered any other police department an option. The MSP was held in high regard by the citizens of Michigan. I had a unique introduction to the state police when I was in high school. It was called a 'Student Trooper Academy,' and somehow, I stumbled upon a poster indicating how to apply. A good friend and I signed up and got accepted.

We attended the week long mini-version of recruit school at the Michigan State Police Academy in Lansing. Our schedule was the same as the recruits. Up at O'dark thirty, intense physical training, intro to law enforcement classes, firearms, the whole nine yards. Upon completing that week of introduction to the MSP, I knew that eventually I was going to wear the sharp blue uniform. Prior to that experience I had no idea about what I wanted to do for a career.

My parents took my buddy and I out for dinner on the way home from Lansing. I told them that I was going to become a state trooper. My dad was stunned. We didn't have anybody in our family who was in law enforcement. My goal had been set. From then on, I pursued it until I received an assignment to the #____ Michigan State Police Recruit School.

The primary appeal to the job was the multitude of ways in which you would be able to help people. I also liked the fact that the MSP had numerous assignments in addition to being a uniformed trooper: K9 handlers, ES Team, fugitive teams, drug teams, detectives, forensic lab positions, and more. For me the MSP was the only option. This was only reinforced when I was later introduced to some troopers. They were the real deal. I knew some other police officers. They had my respect and I knew they did the same job but from what I had seen of the MSP, that's where I was going.

I called recruiters so often, they wished they could change their number, or quit. I pounded on the MSP door so long, and so loud that they eventually had to let me in, if for no other reason than to get me to shut up. Providence eventually landed me in line, in business attire, white long sleeve shirt and tie, in front of the Michigan State Police Academy. Along with the numerous other recruits, I walked into the door ready to go.

I had heard the stories of what awaited me. Hearing and experiencing are two entirely different matters. Many of the recruits would ultimately volunteer to leave. I wasn't going anywhere until I was wearing MSP blue.

PRESSURE

Think of it like a pressure cooker. You walk into the academy as good old you. Then you get cooked for about five months. If you managed to make it to the end and graduate, you walked out of the academy; pressure treated, well trained, and prepared to handle whatever the job was going to throw at you.

Many couldn't handle the stresses. They either quit, got kicked out, or failed the same test twice. Usually during recruit school, there was a guy or two who had previously been through a portion of the academy, but had been unable to finish. There were a few notorious trials to be faced. The guy(s) who experienced those trials, passed along the stories; so, we all got to share in the dread. The major obstacles that we knew awaited us were the boxing program in Defensive Tactics, the water rescue in Water Safety, the precision driving at the drive track, the morning beatings of rigorous workouts, and the ten-mile graduation run.

There were college level classes, and serious physical training, day in and day out. We were permitted to leave Friday evening, and had to return Sunday afternoon. So basically, we had one day off each week. Our academy class started out fairly large, but began to shrink almost immediately as people decided they either could not, or would not tolerate the pressure cooker. I was surprised at how many people started leaving, and how quickly they did.

I had been prepared by MSP troopers, who I knew before the academy. They told me, "You have to walk in through the academy doors with the mindset that the only way you are leaving is if they carry you out. Quitting is not an option, or you will not make it. Either man up and endure the five months, which would likely be the most intense five months of your life, or don't waste their time."

The grinder started even before the first day of the academy. The application process was stout. Written exams with a required minimum grade, psychological exams, drug tests, physical exams, interviews, and waiting. I didn't get my acceptance letter until a few days prior to the start date. I presume it was the same for everyone. They were already stressing us with the "what ifs." Recruiters wouldn't return calls. Inquiries regarding acceptance went unanswered.

Boom. The letter comes in the mail. You have been accepted into the #___ Michigan State Police Recruit School. Guys had other jobs, family, houses, established lives, friendships, etc. Everybody knew that if you graduated, your post assignment would be picked for you, and that could mean having to move across the state.

Reveille blared over the loud speakers at about 5:45a.m. (It's been many years ago, but I believe the time details are correct). P.T. (Physical Training) from 6am-7:15am. The fastest shower you've ever had, and breakfast as fast as you could cram food in your mouth. Run up several flights of stairs, to your floor, and frantically prepare your room for a few minutes before inspection.

INSPECTION

I believe inspection began at 8:00a.m. All the recruits were lined up standing outside of their room, one on either side of the door. Uniformed troopers stepped off the elevator. Slowly they walked by, and inspected everything about you, from the length of your nose hair, to your blue fatigue type uniform.

"Are you looking to hang yourself recruit ___?"

"Sir, no sir!"

"Then why do you have this rope (string) coming out of your shirt button?"

They inspected the military fold of our bed blankets. They would find a piece of lint on the floor, literally. Every time they found anything; we got a mark against us. Usually that meant extra time in a special session for the special people, doing more push-ups, and sit-ups.

Once we were issued our side arms, these too were inspected. They inspected the bathroom and the shower room.

"Who sprayed shaving cream all over (a speck) the bathroom mirror? Who's in charge of the head?"

Every week different recruits would have additional assignments, like making sure the bathroom was clean. If it wasn't, we all paid for it in miles or push-ups.

They inspected our brains for information.

"Recruit ____, who is the Captain of the 2nd District?"

"Sir, I don't know sir."

"You don't know, you could be working for him in a few months, don't you think you should know his name?"

"Sir, yes sir!"

Just when we thought we had sufficiently prepared for questions, they changed them.

"Recruit ____, what is the third step on the Police Use of Force Continuum?"

"Sir, I don't know, sir!"

And it went like this for twenty plus weeks.

Defensive tactics training, water safety, firearms, first aid, traffic law, criminal law, drive training, and more. They ran us from before the sun came up until after the sun went down, and 10pm was lights out. Every night at 10pm we heard the sound of *TAPS* being played over the intercom system. It became a welcome sound. Yet, it was also an omen of things to come; that is the song that is played at police and military funerals. I've heard that song at too many police funerals. We all have.

THE TANK

As anyone can tell by looking at a map, Michigan is surrounded by water. With over 3,000 miles of beach, Michigan is second only to Alaska in this regard. The rigorous water safety program was more than prudent.

The Water Safety portion of the academy lasted for the majority of the school. Much of it was spent trying not to drown. The coursework included lots of time in the tank, that's the designated academy reference to the large indoor pool. We swam laps, treaded water, fetched bricks from the bottom of the tank, learned techniques for various water rescue scenarios, and had an unforgettable experience in ice water. The pinnacle of the water safety program was to rescue an instructor from drowning. This portion of the program had developed a serious reputation of being a formidable gut check.

Occasionally in the morning, after *Reveille*, a trooper would tell us over the intercom system, to report to the stairwell in attire appropriate for P.T. in the tank.

As one might expect, not everybody knows how to swim. Each of the recruits' swimming ability was evaluated by the instructors. The tried and true method to determine how well a person swims, is to have them jump in a pool at the deep end.

"Jump in."

"Sir, I don't know how to swim."

"I don't care, jump in."

"But sir, I don't know how to swim!"

"I don't care! Look around you. Do you see all the floatation devices hanging on the wall?"

"Sir, yes sir!"

"Recruit, do you think I'm gonna let you drown in my tank?!"

"Sir, no sir!"

"Jump in the tank!"

80

The recruit finally jumped in, and what do you know, he couldn't swim. The obedient recruit sank to the bottom of the tank like a rock. Troopers dove in, and brought him to the surface. That recruit had to complete the Water Safety program while wearing inflatable yellow arm floaties. At least he didn't have to use a giant inflatable ducky.

HYPOTHERMIA

A large metal tub had been brought in, which was taller than your average bathtub, and nearly as long. Anyway, it was a tub full to the brim with ice water. There were bags of ice laying on the floor near the tub. I'm guessing one of the troopers got the assignment to buy the entire freezer full from a local gas station.

Several inches of ice floated at the surface. One by one we got to experience what it feels like to be a Narwhal. The impacts of hypothermia upon the human body, are best taught via ice water, rather than in a lecture. We each had to spend four minutes in the icy water. The instructors continually monitored the temperature of the water. They made sure it was about the same as that of Lake Superior, in February.

We had to do dexterity tests at different intervals as we experienced the literal mind-numbing effects of the icy water. The underlying message was clear: don't be a hero and jump into icy water to save somebody unless you can get in and out within two minutes. They taught us the priorities of the rescue options available. Going in was a last resort, even if you could get out quick. Clearly, the best of these options, was to throw a floatation device. In case you were not aware; the back seat of your car comes out, it's foam, and can function as an excellent emergency floatation device.

I watched as muscle bound men trembled in the ice like the leaves in the wind. One of them was a tall, muscular man, without an ounce of fat on him. At the end of four minutes he was physically incapable of getting himself out of the ice filled tub. He had to be helped out by several people. Professional athletes use ice tubs to help reduce inflammation, but I'm fairly certain they don't stay in submerged up to their necks for four minutes.

My turn was like that of the other recruits. There was no testing the waters with your toes, or easing in slowly. Immediate submersion, then remain seated in the iced tub with only your head above the water. My experience with hypothermia was exactly as they said it would be. Blood rushed from my extremities to my core in a subconscious effort to preserve major organs and remain alive. Meanwhile my toes, fingers, legs and arms, all rapidly began to lose feeling. Breathing became labored, and the trembling crescendoed into a violent shaking. One of the happiest moments of my life was getting out of that ice water. Once out of the water I needed help standing so that I didn't fall over.

Afterwards the warming up process was incredibly slow, but it had to be. We stood one at a time, like an assembly line, shivering and shaking while standing within eyeshot of the tub. Then we entered the shower room. Each shower had the temperature incrementally increased, from as cold as it could go, to slightly less cold, to cold, to moderate, to slightly warm, etc. If you didn't go through the process as directed, the water felt like it was boiling when it hit your skin; I tried. Maybe others tried too, but my mind was too frozen to remember. I do recall physical sensations though. Entering even the first cold shower felt hot: it's really incomprehensible unless you've experienced it.

THE RESCUE

There were numerous academy instructors called tempstaff. During the academy, troopers were selected from posts all over the state for this assignment. I'm convinced that some of them were picked purely for their physically imposing physique.

The water rescue involved swimming a few laps, then rescuing the drowning instructor, hauling him down to one end, back to the other, and pulling him out of the water. Like boxing in defensive tactics, this was designed to test one's perseverance and tenacity.

You know that one guy who stands out in a crowd? The guy who nobody ever wants to pick a fight with? The guy whose muscles speak louder than he does? That was the guy I had to rescue.

I had learned to swim at the age of four. My grandma had a cottage on a local lake. My middle school and high school summers were spent there. Occasionally my dream girl from high school, who was a year ahead of me in school, would show up at the public access of the lake. Shake my head; back to reality. Anyway, I knew how to swim.

Years later, I still wonder why that guy was the one I was assigned to rescue. Was it the fact that I knew some troopers prior to the academy? Had they called to try to make the experience more arduous, like some practical joke? It had to be; some ass-hat made a phone call. Why else would 170 pound me draw the biggest most physically intimidating instructor there. Maybe they were still trying to get back at me for hitting a girl, twice (even though they told me to)? Maybe I was supposed to fake hit her, maybe I hit her too hard? Who knows, maybe the giant trooper was who everybody had to rescue, maybe he was hand-picked for that task?

I can see the interview now.

"Alright trooper, your job is to be the guy that everybody has to rescue in the tank. Are you good with that?"

"Sir, yes sir."

"Welcome to temp-staff!"

"Until then, walk around in uniform, with your sleeves rolled up. Slowly pass by each of the recruits every day, when they are standing in line. Make sure you're close enough that they can smell your breath and see the glare shining off of your shoes."

The dreaded day came. I waited my turn in the hallway until my name was called. I was rushed into the room, told to dive in and swim a few lengths of the pool. Then on one of my trips back to the deep end, I saw him. The trooper with the rolled-up sleeves, and minty breath, was just waiting at the deep end. He was acting like he was drowning, and it was my skinny ass who was supposed to save him.

They say that a drowning victim will panic, and do anything including drowning a would-be rescuer by trying to climb on top of them. I got to experience this. The bicep of colossus squashed my face, and his giant arm squeezed my head. He may have been trying to see if it would pop off. All of this while I was under water. I remember thinking if he doesn't let go, I'm not getting out of this, but I still struggled like hell to free myself.

Eventually he decided that he shouldn't drown me and loosened his grip enough that I could wiggle out. I dragged him the length of the pool and back and tried to haul his big ass out of the deep end of the tank. It had to be a ridiculous sight watching some 170-pound young punk trying to pull the 250-pound hulk out of the tank. Maybe that's why they chose him; for sheer entertainment value.

The grand finale rescue was precisely the gut check it was reputed to be.

TEAR GAS

In the academy all of the recruits were required to run through a cloud of tear gas. I had no idea what to expect, but I knew it wouldn't be pleasant. The stories of soldiers experiencing this are occasionally told over a cold beer, but words cannot do it justice.

A canister of tear gas was released on a windy day. There was a large white smoky cloud blowing downwind. We were all on one side of the cloud and instructed to run through it to the other side: "It can't be that bad, just run..." I thought.

We entered the blinding fog, which caused a unique burning sensation to our eyes, as we tried to find our way through to the other side. The particles in the air entered our lungs. The whole experience was disorientating. People in the cloud began to stop, suffering from, trouble breathing, impaired vision, and panic.

Some pushed the stalled recruits through, some pulled. We were a blinded, gagging, discombobulated mess. Some recruits couldn't even make it through to the other side. They entered the cloud, and were so overcome by the experience that they turned back. The gas disorients, temporarily blinds, inhibits breathing, and induces a panic-like effect. The human body reacts to the nasty substance by immediately summoning all mucus reserves to the mouth and nose.

No sinus infection or bronchitis could ever compare with the fountain of snot the body pours out, trying to cleanse itself from that gas. I have never watched snot pour from my nose and mouth like that. It wasn't thin, but gaggingly thick and voluminous. I didn't know the body could produce that much mucus, nor that it could do so instantly.

I made my way through the cloud, maybe twenty or thirty feet. I thought it was over. No, it was just beginning. I looked around and saw snot hanging from the faces of recruits, bending over instinctively to allow the mucus to run its choking route. I coughed and gagged. My eyes burned, and my lungs hacked. My stomach would have emptied itself through my mouth as well, except that my superhero power is the ability not to vomit. Several people around me were puking. Some were laying on the ground, simply overcome.

The faucet of snot had been turned all the way open. I gagged and half-panicked as I choked on the gluey mess clogging my throat. All I could do, all we could do, was let the body do its thing. If we were not all in the same position, we were all in the same physical condition; trying not to die by choking on snot.

It was a learning experience for sure. But I didn't think I'd ever be around if and when it was used. At that point I hadn't encountered situations or events which would require tear gas to be launched into marauding crowds.

The instructors weren't introducing us to the experience for nothing. The department had reasons for providing us with gas masks and repetitive practice in how to use them.

It was years later when the time came to use the mask. The order was given and the gas mask was on within a minute. I was breathing through my filter, and glad that I wasn't one of the rioters without it.

It was near midnight and the streets were covered with angry people. Numerous canisters of the gas were shot into the mob. People tried to cover their faces with their clothes, but it was pointless. One minute they were all crowded together and feeding off of the energy from each other. The next minute they were running for their lives, trying to escape the asphyxiating fog. They scattered like birdshot from a shotgun.

Our academy class got to experience one canister, in the daylight. The rioters experienced the intensity of about a dozen cans of gas at night. The streets were cleared. Problem solved.

DEFENSIVE TACTICS

The UFC (Ultimate Fighting Championship) was gaining traction around the time I went through the academy. The instructors had trained with some big names of that time.

Ground fighting apparently seemed like a good idea, to at least introduce us to. Having been an average wrestler in middle school and high school, I knew that a lot of practice would be necessary to become proficient at this. I also knew, from watching a few professional boxing matches and being a fan of the UFC, that even champs can get knocked out if caught with a good punch. Professional fighters, who train constantly for a living, can get choked out in the ground game.

The instructors were generally solid individuals with different backgrounds, military, martial arts, etc. They were often the type of guys that you wouldn't want to step into the octagon with. But not all troopers or officers can compete in that arena. Even the toughest of officers could go down with a well thrown punch.

During my freshman year in high school wrestling, I watched a senior from another school and in another weight class during numerous matches. He had a reputation, for good reason. The dude was tough. I had seen him at tournaments and when our team would wrestle his. In wrestling, only the best developed reputations. These were the guys whose names were known at every school within thirty miles. Anyway, I met him later as an adult, and I knew he had trained hard in mixed martial arts. You couldn't pay me to get into the ring with that guy.

He told me a story about one of his training days. He was working out when a notorious boxer from the area entered the gym. Some guys told him not to do it, but he ended up in the ring with the dude who was a wicked boxer. The boxer told him repeatedly to keep his hands up. Apparently, they traded a few punches. Then the wrestler woke up, on his back. He said he'd never been hit so hard.

Even badasses can get throttled. Every champ loses their belt at some point. The professionals aren't perfect. That's why all the pre-fight talk is meaningless. Anybody can get beat on any given day.

However, the academy defensive tactics (D.T.) instructors didn't say any of this. I don't know if they were trying to keep our confidence up, or just not scare the shit out of us. Maybe they simply wanted to give us what they had, with the limited time available, and hope for the best? While they were teaching, I knew they knew. It would have been impossible for them not to.

I had come to the conclusion then that I wasn't the biggest, nor the baddest, and that if someone was going to physically come after me, they'd be facing down the barrel of my pistol. I knew that going to the gun could be a rapid decision.

You never know what the bad guy's background is. He could have been a state champ wrestler, or a golden gloves boxer, someone who is just plain tougher than you, or some nobody who lands a lucky punch. You also never know what his motivation is; he could have thousands of dollars of drugs in the car, a pocket full of heroin, or on parole and doesn't want to go back to prison.

Some officers are afraid of escalating too quickly. They're concerned about prosecution, lawsuits, jail, etc. Sometimes there isn't time to go first to the spray, second to the baton, third to the taser, and finally to the gun. In certain situations, immediate escalation to the level of potentially fatal force is the only option. This is easy to see if you've watched any police videos, especially police training videos (real incidents that not all of the public has access to).

In my career, out of everyone who I physically struggled with, only one directed his aggression at me physically. Everybody else was just struggling to get away. In all of my years of police work, in all of the areas I worked, in the rural areas and the city environments; just that one individual purposefully acted aggressively towards me. If someone comes at you, not away from you (though you need to be careful with them as well), a cop must be able to escalate very fast. Aggression directed at an officer is illegal to begin with, and automatically puts the officer's life at risk. One of the biggest issues regarding assaults on officers is that there's always a gun in the fight. Many officers have been killed with their own weapon.

Most police officers aren't body builders. Even the ones who are can be throttled, given the right opponent. Being in shape was necessary for foot chases, wrestling matches, and other such encounters with suspects. However, an officer's mind is his most effective weapon. They have to recognize when things are about to go sideways. They must be willing to escalate action rapidly in order to deal with situations when necessary. The goal was to go home at the end of your shift. That meant doing what is needed, when it is needed.

I wasn't concerned about pulling the trigger if necessary. That ideological bridge was one that I crossed while at the academy. At one point, I recall struggling with the idea of having to take the life of another. It was a make it or break it decision, as to whether this career was the right choice for me. I thought about it for several days and came to the conclusion that if I ever had to pull the trigger; it would be in order to save the life of another, or my own.

ONE OF THE MOST HELPFUL LESSONS FROM D.T.

This training came later in my career, well after the academy. It was regarding securing a subject in handcuffs. It was this technique which was referred to earlier in the book, under the heading *"SCHWACK!!!"*

This method was much more practical, and realistic than the prior method I had learned in the academy. An officer has the subject place his hands behind his back and interlock his fingers together. While directing people to do this, many officers often describe the folding of the hands, "As if you were praying." Though I presume that not many of those being handcuffed are in the habit of praying.

Firmly grip the subject's interlocked fingers, with your support hand. This locks their fingers/knuckles together.

A solid grip on the subject gives you a bit more time to react if the suspect decides to try to get away or fight. It's taught to officers that generally if a suspect is going to fight or attempt to get away, they will often do so at the moment of the first physical contact. Action is quicker than reaction, and a few extra seconds in such a situation might just save your life.

RECRUIT SCHOOL THESIS

The academy was a finely tuned training machine, which transformed recruits into troopers. I have developed an affinity for summary overviews, which can be especially helpful in literature. The idea is that a particular set of information can be boiled down to a thesis sentence or two. Contemplating the five difficult months at the MSP academy, has left me with the impression that the primary thesis of the training was; "Never quit."

Every morning prior to P.T., recruits would line up against a wall. Prominently hung on the wall in front of us was a large sign on which was written the phrase, "If you think you can, you will. If you think you can't, your right." The instructors would have us yell the phrase, often repeatedly before we ran into the gym. We did this so often that the words on that sign have been burned into my memory.

It wasn't only the sign, or the daily echo of about one-hundred recruits shouting its message. "Never quit" was hammered into our psyche in lesson after lesson; from pushups, pull-ups, and extremely long runs, to boxing someone hand-picked to beat your ass, rescuing the hulk from drowning, to first aid and the intellectual challenges of college level classes. During some of the physically challenging portions of defensive tactics, the instructor would yell things like, "Are you gonna quit on me? Are you gonna quit on your partner? Are you gonna quit when some huge logger wants to take your gun?"

Day after day they pushed us to our physical limits then they pushed us further. Daily we learned that our minds can force our bodies to go on, when our bodies were screaming that we couldn't. Verbally and physically the lesson was branded upon our hearts.

The Navy SEALs experience this to an extraordinarily higher degree. Their ethos includes the phrase, "I am never out of the fight."[4] The famous Navy SEAL, who was known for ending Bin Laden, often autographs his book, *The Operator*, next to the words, "Never Quit."

CUB

New troopers were called cubs. I found it offensive and disrespectful after having just gone through the hell of the MSP academy. I wore the same uniform they did, and would respond to the same calls for service as them. At one point I heard a trooper say, "You're not a trooper until you've done the job for at least five years." Again, I was offended. By that time, I had seen some of the competition in blue and knew that I could hang with them in just about any situation. Yet it was crystal clear that there were other guys, with whom this was not the case. I knew that it would take me years to reach their level of proficiency in this job, which has a massive learning curve.

After about five years on the job, I admit I finally saw the truth in that trooper's statement

---

[4] Marcus Lutrell, *Lone Survivor*, and navyseals.com

"They say money is the root of all evil. If it's not ALL, it's pretty damn close."

Chapter Six

METH

A PLAGUE ON SOCIETY

Meth is, in my opinion, the most devastating of all illicit narcotics. This drug has a horrible impact on the health of many children, as it is often cooked at home and in their presence. Extremely toxic chemicals are involved in the cooking process; this has a devastating impact upon the environment. It is also a major fire hazard.

Easy access to an over-the-counter decongestant has contributed to the widespread use of meth across this country. At least one state that I am aware of has made pseudo-ephedrine a controlled drug, requiring a prescription. This has put a massive road block in the meth problem there.

One allergy pill, is the primary source of the meth epidemic in America. The simple act of requiring buyers to have a prescription (as they had been previously), would handcuff the meth problem, overnight.

Command officers know this.

Therefore, law makers know it as well.

The inescapable conclusion is that the pharmaceutical companies do also.

Corporate greed is responsible for this epidemic.

METH FIRE

My cell phone rang in the middle of the night. I answered, still half-asleep.

There'd been a meth fire, a suspect/burn victim was at the hospital. My boss instructed me to go there and interview him.

I headed out right away. The hospital was a good distance away, and I wanted to get there before the suspect was discharged.

I later found that the suspect had been significantly burned, and wasn't going anywhere anytime soon. A female subject was there also. She did not have any injuries but she was detained as a possible suspect. Neither one of them wanted to talk. The female subject finally confessed that the fire was meth-related. However, they would not say where it happened. The investigation was stalled for a while as I tried to determine the location by interviewing the two.

An experienced trooper had previously introduced me to the concept of what he called having a "silver tongue." On a few different occasions I witnessed him smooth talk his way into suspect confessions, searches, and more. He became officer nice guy, really nice guy. He compassion-ed information out of people, many of whom did not want to provide the information. That trooper talked his way into minds and hearts.

Having watched him work his magic a few times, I started to practice the art of the silver tongue. Sometimes leverage works, sometimes the nice guy routine works. A well-known phrase captures the basic idea; you catch more bees with honey. The silvery honey eventually worked on the female. She finally gave up the location and even showed us the way; physically pointing out the house.

The team was notified. Guys started showing up one by one, initially at the hospital. I drafted a search warrant which was authorized by a judge. We donned our meth lab response gear including gas masks. Into the house we went. The third suspect was in the home with two young children as well. They were removed by social workers.

A meth lab was discovered and evidence of the fire. Meth-related paraphernalia was found throughout the home. An abundance of previously used meth lab components was located nearby.

The three suspects were arrested. The mother of the children was also located and arrested. Despite already having a mountain of evidence, I interviewed all of them. Each confessed to felony meth charges. I called a few federal agents and they gladly got involved. Two of the suspects ended up in federal prison, the others got state or county time.

ONE BURNING DESIRE

Farmers regularly have large quantities of a particular fertilizer which meth makers often use to cook the horrible substance with. The liquid fertilizer was so often stolen that we began to set alarms on the large portable containers at various farms. The highly sought-after fertilizer is toxic to humans in several ways. If it comes into contact with skin it would cause terrible burns and if it's inhaled, lungs can be severely and permanently damaged.

On a cloudless winter night shift with a brilliant moon, my partner and I decided to go check on some of these farms. The moon was sufficiently bright for us to be able to see well enough to drive without the headlights on. The light cover of snow on the ground combined with the giant nightlight in the sky provided for excellent visibility.

We observed a van parked near one of the fertilizer tanks. It was easily two or three hundred yards away. We parked in the middle of the road, partially hidden by some trees and waited. In the distance a few people were barely visible committing the crime. Then the headlights of the van turned on and it began driving directly at us. They had no clue.

The plan was to attempt to stop them from the front by hitting the emergency lights with plenty of distance for them to stop. We were parked in the center of both lanes of the road, not entirely closing off a potential escape route.

Things often don't go exactly as planned. When we hit the lights, they didn't stop. I could see them toss something of substantial size out of the side of the van onto the shoulder.

They got around us only because we didn't feel like denting our snazzy blue ride. The old full-size van wasn't gonna get away, we just gave them a head start to give them a temporary morale boost. We spun around and the chase was on. They didn't get too far before their vehicle slid off of the snowy road, and into the ditch.

We carefully secured each of the three occupants, one of whom had serious burns on his hands and arms. The van was left with the doors open to air it out, and the meth response team was called out to assist. (This was one of the responsibilities which came with an assignment to a drug team.)

The object that the suspects had tossed out of the van was a standard size propane tank, which the suspects had used to hold the toxic liquid fertilizer. When propane tanks were used for this purpose the nozzles would become a distinct bluish color.

The three subjects had been caught red handed, one literally. Three people with felony charges equals rapid fire information about many other meth cooks and criminals. They were anxious to do whatever they could to get out of hot water, and into slightly less hot water.

The information they provided, led to search warrants at a few suspect residences. All of the interviews, necessary paperwork, search warrants, and more culminated in what was the longest shift of my career. It was over twenty hours.

The department eventually set the maximum limit at sixteen hours per shift.

Meth-heads are relentless in the pursuit of their habit. However, a tremendous number of police officers are just as relentless in their battle against this pestilence.

THE GREEN MONSTER

They say that money is the root of all evil. If it's not *all,* it's pretty damn close. Greed lines the pockets of too many politicians, and purchases their influence.

Meth labs are expensive to tackle because of the severity of inherent environmental concerns. It is costly to deal with this toxic substance, although it seems that less expensive means could be developed.

There are some tools which legislators have provided to law enforcement, which could have resulted in the arrest of untold numbers of meth cooks, and those who supply them. However, these have largely been rendered inert by department budgets which struggle to keep up with the expenses of meth lab cleanup.

"I sat there, waiting in the car, in the dark. My semi-automatic pistol was readily accessible. It provided some level of comfort in the rather uncomfortable situation..."

Chapter Seven

UNDERCOVER

APPLICATION PROCESS

There is a selection process for troopers who want to transition from uniform into a specialty team. The first step in the process to be considered for such an assignment, was a letter of request providing reasons why you would be a suitable applicant. This letter would initially be forwarded to a First Lieutenant, referred to as a Post Commander or PC.

The whole letter idea seemed to be an unnecessary formality to me. Everyone who applies is going to write the same thing:

Greetings, name, time in rank. Sir I've been an MSP trooper, like everybody else in the department is. I've done what good troopers do, etc.

It was almost humorous. What really mattered was what the boss said. You could have a letter written by Mark Twain himself and in golden ink, but if the boss says no then you could flush Twain's artistic rendition.

An endorsement from the PC was required for the application process to continue. If for whatever reason, the boss didn't approve, the process ended there. Upon receiving the approval of the PC, the letter was then sent up the chain of command to one of the highest commanding officers in the MSP, in this case a Lieutenant Colonel.

If the Lt. Col. approved, an applicant was scheduled for an interview before three commanding officers in the District (a large area consisting of numerous MSP Posts).

So there I sat at a table across from three commanding officers, in a room at District HQ. I knew each of the three men across the table from me. Two of them were Sergeants at different worksites where I had previously been assigned. The other was known only by name and face, as he was a supervising officer on a specialty team in the same district for many years.

Each had unique questions, and each were able to cross examine my responses if they chose. It was the first time I had ever interviewed for any position. After the barrage of questions was complete, I was dismissed. It seemed to have gone well, but I wasn't sure in light of the fact that I had nothing to compare it to.

If I recall correctly, a phone call came about a week or two later, from the commanding officer of the drug team.

"Congratulations. One of the guys will pick you up at your place in the morning."

I got to hang up my uniforms for a while. After about a decade or so of wearing them, I was happy to leave them in my locker at the post. While I'd miss the tough blue Dodge Chargers with the red bubble on top, I looked forward to the unmarked UC take-home ride.

LONG HAIRED FREAKY PEOPLE

Uniformed troopers have requirements as to how long their hair can be. Facial hair was limited to an eighties style mustache, neat and trim. Most of my career was spent in uniform, so I was always the clean-cut guy that ladies didn't worry about at the bank or in a grocery store.

In non-uniform positions, for the most part, appearances are entirely unhindered. In some of these assignments, the whole idea is to not look like a cop. Most guys got grungy, but some only ventured a little off the reservation.

During a day off, I was walking into a bank, and a lady who I had known on a first name basis for years was walking out. She looked at me and clutched her purse tight. I said her name, and she was a bit stunned, it took her a minute to recognize me. This happened on a few occasions with people who I had known, but hadn't seen in a while. Another such occasion happened at the same bank with an old friend.

Anyway, I chose the grungy route. The reservation had long since disappeared in my rearview mirror. Now I was the guy who made ladies walk so close to the other side of the aisle as to barely avoid knocking items off of the shelves. Little did they know I was the same guy who used to be clean cut and in a uniform. I was carrying a gun tucked under my shirt, but it was legally, and not for robbing people in the parking lot.

It's interesting to observe the reactions of people, and how much they change simply because of your outward appearance. I guess people play the odds. Judging by appearance, we presume that guy is probably a dirt-bag. Meanwhile the nice guy in the suit behind us in the checkout aisle is the one we should be concerned about. Books and their covers can be remarkably different.

PROFILED

I was headed back to the office to do some paperwork, after having just purchased a small baggie of cocaine. While on the way, I observed a sheriff's department patrol car. Evidently the deputy had observed grungy me, and my equally grungy ride. He initiated a traffic stop and I pulled into a parking lot off of the road.

The deputy came to my window and didn't recognize me. While I was getting my real ID, my boss pulled up within ear shot. He yelled to the deputy something like, you might want to search that guy, I'll bet you'll find something.

I told him who I was and showed my identification. He hadn't recognized me, but I'm pretty sure he recognized my boss.

LITTLE FISH, BIGGER FISH

Informants were not in short supply. They either were looking to potentially work off some charges, or for revenge against rivals. Officers from multiple different agencies would send us the info on the informant and the situation. Those looking to flip info on someone else, do buys themselves, and/or intro a long hair like me.

A trooper I had previously worked with, had flipped me a guy who could walk me into his coke dealer's home. It wasn't really a home it was a one-bedroom apartment that housed two or three guys. Apparently, some cocaine dealers don't make a whole lot of money.

Anyway, the informant provided the information. A plan was made, and the team was all set to do their job. My guy walked in first and I followed. There wasn't much to see in what could barely be called a studio apartment. I did however get a good look at the two guys inside. The deal went down quickly. I talked to the easy-going dealer for a minute and told him that if it was good, I'd be back for more.

His cocaine tested positively in the little plastic test pack. Within a few days I called up the dealer and arranged for another purchase of the same amount, which was about 150 dollars. The second deal didn't require the informant to be there. I got to speak to the guy again for a few minutes, and got another quick look around the small room.

As I walked outside, a guy was walking inside with a brown package which was partially wrapped in tape. I had a pretty good idea what was inside. The size was noteworthy. It wasn't the standard kilo size. I had encountered several of those on the road, before the undercover assignment. It was more like the size of a quarter kilo.

My boss and I discussed the option of hitting the door, in case I was right about the package. We concluded that if they were moving that kind of weight it would be around again, and we'd let this play out a bit.

After a week or so I called again. This time I arranged for a greater quantity. The increased amount also increased the criminal charge to a higher-level felony. We had to pull some strings to get the extra cash needed for the purchase.

It was during that case that I first heard the name of an agency which provides big money if needed. They also had a broad range of technological equipment, and other such things to assist law enforcement. That agency had to be contacted in order for our team to fund the deal. I filled out the application for the cash. A short while later, our team received a check from this agency in the amount requested.

The boss-man told me to go cash the check. This too was new territory. I went to a nearby bank and asked to speak with a manager. I got some odd looks in light of my dirt-bag appearance and unusual request. Imagine how the manager reacted, it was just about like that. I sat in an office for a while. Phone calls were made, and eventually I walked out of the bank with the most money I'd ever held in my hands.

Upon returning to the office, I made another recorded phone call to the suspect and firmed up details of the arrangement. He said he'd meet me at the same place. With the team set to go, we headed out to do the deal. As I was driving to the location, I received a phone call from the suspect. He wanted to change plans. Bigger dope means bigger money and more potential for trouble. The suspect wanted me to go to a house fifteen or twenty miles away from the place where we had made the previous deals. That residence had recently come up on our radar screen. This request added confirmation to our info on the house.

Safety was the concern, and my boss didn't like the change in plans. He called and told me to arrange for the deal at the original location, or call it off. I called the guy back and explained that I wanted to deal with him, and didn't want to bring my cash to a location I wasn't familiar with. We pushed back and forth. But ultimately it was the money that did the talking. The suspect wasn't gonna walk away from several thousand dollars. He agreed to meet at the same place. I told him I'd wait out front.

Our previous deals had occurred during daylight. The suspect waited until after dark for this deal to go down. I parked in front of the shabby residence in which his apartment was located. There were no lights on in the home. The area along the small side street was dark except for a street light a half block away.

The guy knew I had big cash. It was the biggest cash deal our team had done while I was assigned there. In the scheme of UC deals, it wasn't that big. In fact, years prior I had worked with a UC team who was buying a kilo of cocaine. I was one of the uniformed guys involved, and my role was to stop the suspect as he drove away after the deal.

The UC was a dirty longhair that looked like anything but a police officer. I could listen in on the deal, it was a learning experience. That UC should have taught classes in how to be successful in the unique assignment. His deal went down, the suspect drove away and immediately got to meet me and another uniformed trooper. Done like dinner.

My case was nowhere close to the size of that one, but it was a solid case nonetheless. I sat there, waiting in my car, in the dark. My semi-automatic pistol was readily accessible. It provided some level of comfort in the rather uncomfortable situation.

A male subject was walking towards me. He was coming from the opposite direction where I expected the suspect to come from. He was a hundred yards or so down the street, across from the front of his apartment. I called out the only description I had; a male subject in a hoodie. He had the hood pulled down low and I couldn't see his face until he was almost at my door.

It was him. He handed me a package. It was approximately the size of two golf balls, and was wrapped in aluminum foil. We exchanged a few words and I gave him the cash. He didn't count the money and I didn't inspect the package. It would have been a good idea to do so, but I wasn't gonna take my eyes off of him.

We parted ways. It was only a short while later that uniformed troopers were requested to stop his car, they did so and the dealer was placed under arrest and transported to the jail. The boss was pleased to see that we had gotten the cash back as planned.

Border patrol got a call from me about that suspect. He was in the States illegally. I knew that the agents were plenty busy and that they had a policy of not bothering with people who only had misdemeanor charges. But a guy with a few felony charges was another story. I'm not sure how it all played out, but I know this much; the suspect got locked up and was eventually deported. I played a primary role criminally charging about a dozen people who ended up being deported for felony charges. Not all of these were for drug charges, but the majority were.

Sometimes tossing the little fish back, results in a bigger fish in the frying pan.

E-DEALING

The advertisement for marijuana was posted on Craigslist by an enterprising individual. At the time, Michigan's medical marijuana law allowed for a licensed grower to sell the product to a limited number of "patients." I wasn't this guy's patient, but that didn't stop him from working his side gig.

We arranged to meet in the parking lot of a local business. The lot was covered by video surveillance. The entrepreneurial twenty-something white guy was punctual for his business deals. I walked up to his car, and sat in the passenger seat. We spoke briefly and he showed me the weed. I was happy with the product and paid the man.

The suspect was quickly identified. A bit of investigation revealed that he was an out-of-state resident who was trying to cash in on the Michigan medical marijuana law.

Afterwards my boss explained to me the foolishness of getting into the passenger seat of a suspect's car during a deal. Not only was the guy committing a felony, if he took off with you in the car, things could go south. What if the team lost you? Anyway, his point was well taken, and I wouldn't make that mistake again.

I arranged for another buy from the same guy. We met and I purchased the few illegal products he was selling. I said the magic words that the team was waiting for, then the suspect got a quick introduction to the rest of the crew. He seemed startled by how quickly he was snatched out of the car and cuffed.

On his scale of morality, cash outweighed the potential consequences of committing felonies. It was a common theme among people we dealt with: cash is king. He wasn't the only guy our team caught by advertising some controlled substances via the internet.

INFORMANT

Some officers constantly worked at developing informants. Once their suspects chose the happy road of trying to work off some charges, they got to meet one of us. I was up to bat and got a guy who was gonna work with me on a meth buy. We waited until dark because meth-heads, like vampires, don't like the sun.

So, these two unsavory characters walk into a bar. Actually, it was to my car, and I drove to the predetermined location. It wasn't the type of place where you'd have a butler awaiting your arrival, open your door and carry your jacket.

We parked outside and remained in the car. After a while, a white male came out of the trailer and walked up to my door. Meth-heads aren't known to be upstanding citizens and this particular meth-head knew I was coming with some money. I didn't like the fact that I couldn't see his hands, but was prepared to deal with the situation if things went south.

We talked for a minute and he said, "You're not a cop, are you?" I answered with my standard line, "Do I fucking look like a cop." It is widely rumored among such malcontents that if you ask, a police officer has to tell you if he is a cop. That may or may not be a rumor perpetuated by undercover cops.

The meth supplier was hospitable and invited us into his trailer. I avoided the invite with some nonsense excuse about time. The real reason I didn't want to go into his trailer is that I didn't know if he was cooking meth in there.

Our training included explicit details of how toxic the whole meth making process is. The chemicals involved are bad enough, but the act of cooking the substance is volatile. The plastic pop bottles which are often used as the oven would occasionally explode with a fiery blast, not unlike a Molotov cocktail.

The suspect eventually indicated that he was fresh out of the marketable commodity, but he had called a buddy who would bring some. Meth friends are pals as long as there's meth or cash around, and they're anything but reliable. They say, there's no honor among thieves. There's even less among meth-people.

While reliability may be a problem for those who use and sell meth, it is not a problem for cops. Especially among teams that rely on each other in case the SHTF.

Finally, my informant's dealer's supplier showed up. Great, more people present who know I've got cash in the car. That's ok. I had people in the area as well. The kind that wear body armor and have big guns.

The meth buddy proved to be in need of cash, and gave his small package to my new and hospitable friend. I handed him some cash, he handed me some meth.

"I gotta go. Hey, I know a cook, maybe I can bring him next time." I drove away with the meth in hand.

Next time never came. But a felony warrant for delivering meth did. We waited a while to arrest the suspect in order that he might have a difficult time identifying the inform-ant. Not that it mattered. His rather long criminal history record plus the felony meth charge sent him back to prison for a while.

I went home that night and told my wife, "Honey I bought my first meth today."

She said, "Oh I'm so proud of you," and gave me a hug.

BUNK

A motivated officer flipped a suspect over to me, who al-legedly could intro me to his cocaine dealer.

The informant, bad guy #1, was a regular resident of the jail. He screwed around with the cops enough that he was lucky to have gotten another opportunity. If we had access to a fraction of what he knew, we could have significantly interfered with the local drug problem. He was a criminal, but he wasn't dumb. He'd toss us a low-level player.

We all knew he could bring bigger cases, but he knew bet-ter than to tip his hand regarding the higher level. We were gonna have to toss a decent sized trout back in for a bluegill.

I took his low-level guy. Sometimes the smaller guys would rather flip on a bigger guy, rather than take a felony charge.

Bad guy #1 was trying to work off a traffic related charge, so we'd take a felony case over that. My boss was familiar with the informant and disliked him enough that he almost refused to work with him.

I met up with bad guy #1, who introduced me to his guy, bad guy #2. As happened on occasion, we had to wait for a third party to bring the package. I waited with bad guys #1 and #2, always keeping them both in view. I certainly didn't trust the informant. Not that I trust anybody anyways, but there are people like him who are miles beyond untrustworthy.

The clock ticked, and I kept sizing up the two of them, thinking about what I'd do first if things went sideways. I was aware of the well-known phrase, "Everybody's got a plan until they get punched in the mouth." Yet it didn't hurt to have plan B and C in mind.

My guy's, guy's, guy eventually showed up. Bad guy #3 delivered the clear plastic baggie of a white powdery substance to guy #2, who sold it to me for a fistful of twenties. Now we had another suspect, and the surveillance crew did their job and identified suspect #3.

Once I could field test the substance, I found that it wasn't positive for cocaine. It turned out to be crushed up drywall. Wise guy#3 thought he was getting away with something by getting my cash in exchange for nothing. He probably didn't realize it's also illegal to sell imitation narcotics. Felony warrants were sought for both guys.

On this occasion, the fish we tossed back resulted in two more fish in the bucket.

QUICK ON HIS BOOTS

One of the most advantageous characteristics of a UC was to be able to think fast on your feet. This was something I did not have. I had no trouble making quick calls in uniform. In the UC position, I had to plan what I would say or do in certain situations. I am analytical, and like to view situations from different vantage points to come up with the best option. But that's entirely different from being alone in the midst of felons, and being able to talk your way out of trouble. If you were good at spinning quick lines of BS, you had one of the most necessary skills to be a good UC. I worked with guys who were like me, and had to develop verbal contingency plans beforehand.

There was however one guy who excelled in this area. He talked himself deeper into cases he was investigating, while he was doing buys. This guy had no need to pre-plan his words. He could spin BS like one of the people on Drew Carey's show, "*Whose Line is it Anyway*?" Officer Improv, talked his way into situations I never could have. He had some great war stories, and I got to witness several of them. The team was generally able to listen in on a UC deal, and his improv was impressive. Except for one occasion.

He was rightly confident in his slippery tongue. However, during one incident his confidence may have gotten the best of him. I was with the team listening to him as he arranged the buy. Then the subject who he was dealing with, noticed he had police boots on, and called him on it. No amount of the UC's BS could sway the nervous dealer. The suspect shut the deal down, and business was closed there for a while.

INSPECTOR GADGETS

Our team had a few gadgets up our sleeve to work with. I did some quick internet searching, and discovered more. The boss was notified, and our arsenal of tricky technology increased.

The new tech equipment was up to date, and proved very useful. Our video capabilities improved, and we obtained some of our own tracking devices. These were items we previously only had access to by contacting one of our MSP tech guys. That equipment was in high demand all over the state, but since these items were easy enough to use, we got our own. They weren't the quality of Q's innovations for Bond, but they were stealthy and worthwhile. The prosecutor liked seeing the faces of the suspects on video, even during night deals. On more than a few occasions, I'd have to go with a partner in the wee hours of the morning and retrieve a tracking device from a vehicle.

On one occasion I placed the device on a vehicle after it was involved in a solid drug case, from a traffic stop. We watched where it went for a while. It ended up in a rough neighborhood in Detroit, and I had to go and retrieve it. I had contacted a local drug team in D-town, who agreed to provide backup. It was around 3:00a.m. when I arrived. My car was parked far enough away to avoid drawing suspicion in the area where the subject vehicle was parked.

With my gun tucked in my waistband, and a hoodie pulled well over my head, I walked toward the objective. The car was parked in the driveway of a two-story residence. There was a street light not far from the house. Shadows are your friend in these situations. I crawled under the vehicle, to where I had originally placed the device. It was secured a little too well. I spent a few minutes under the car working on the project. The backup crew contacted me via a silenced cellphone and asked what was taking so long. I pulled a knife out of my pocket and used it to leverage the tracker loose. I hated having to use that knife for such a purpose, but it worked.

The device was placed in my hoodie pocket and I rolled out from underneath the vehicle, checking to see if I was in the clear. Nobody was visible in the area. I advised the crew that I had the item, and walked back to my car. Once I drove out of the area, I thanked the crew for watching my six, and travelled a few hours back home.

THE PRO'S

Word had got out that we had some tracking devices. A buddy from another department gave me some good intel on a guy they were looking at, and asked for help. The suspect usually kept his car in the garage, but for some reason it was parked in the driveway that night, so we took advantage of the opportunity. Two deputies came with me as back-up while I secured the device onto the vehicle.

The suspect was a middle-aged man who had been popped years earlier for moving a significant quantity of marijuana. Apparently, he had learned some things along the way, because he was still in the game. Several officers had him on their radar screens. The tracking device worked well, and provided some good intel.

A storage unit complex and a local business with excellent video surveillance were identified as recent destinations. I obtained a copy of the digital video, which showed the man buying one item, a box of gallon-sized zip-lock bags. These are commonly used to contain about a pound of marijuana. Then another officer and I travelled to the storage units. We contacted the manager and gave him a name. Sure enough, the suspect was renting one of the units.

After having obtained the storage unit number, I contacted our K9 team to assist. The dog indicated positively on the storage shed. I drafted a search warrant, which was authorized by one of the local judges. We gathered up a few guys and went to search the storage unit.

Based on all of this information, none of us were surprised to find what we did. There was a decent amount of marijuana inside. It was an upper level dealer quantity. Another search warrant was obtained, and we searched the man's residence, but it was clean. He knew how to do business. He'd been in the game for decades. There are numerous other noteworthy details about how he did business, but that information certainly shouldn't be passed along to the public. He was a professional, but sometimes even the pro's get beat.

His travel destinations included some out-of-state trips. Federal agents were contacted and were happy to get involved. While facing some heavy felony marijuana charges, the suspect was willing to provide some information.

The deputy who initially contacted me about this case was glad to hear that the guy finally got caught.

The trackers were helpful on several cases. One of the inexpensive devices may or may not have been lost on another case. If it was, I don't know if it would have been reported, nor do I know if a particular supervisor would even have noticed. That is of course, if it ever even happened.

I ALWAYS FEEL LIKE, SOMEBODY'S WATCHING ME

The surveillance class was one of the more interesting and action packed, of the numerous training classes I had during my career. The first portion was classroom instruction on the basics. Then the rest was practice.

We may or may not have driven around Michigan surveilling instructors during different scenarios. We worked primarily on vehicle surveillance, but we also did some brief suspect tailing on foot. The training was extremely helpful.

As an undercover officer, we always worked with a team. Each of us had specialized training classes relevant to the UC assignment. Basically, we all did the same thing, and had the identical training.

In real world situations, we spent much time surveilling suspects. It generally involved long periods of waiting and boredom. The waiting did however provide time to increase my proficiency in flinging little birds at green pigs. When the suspect was moving, things got interesting. City venues and rural areas each presented unique benefits and difficulties. The cities provided plenty of traffic to blend into, but the traffic became as much of an obstacle as it was cover. Rural areas provided a different set of pros and cons.

The movies don't show surveillance crews playing *Clash of the Clans*. However, when we were doing the real thing, such diversions were the life preservers that saved us from drowning in boredom.

Our team was occasionally called upon to assist other agencies with some of their cases that didn't involve narcotics. They were serious felony cases. Each resulted in the eventual arrest of the suspect.

Some cases were from out of state. Occasionally an agency from across the country would have hemmed up some suspect(s) with significant charges. Those people would flip on their contacts in our neck of the woods. We had a few interesting cases which involved big money and/or drugs, and a few different surveillance crews.

Occasionally, a suspect would live far enough away from a main road that somebody was needed on foot, to get an eye on the suspect residence and vehicles. On one such occasion, I volunteered for this duty. It was a cold wintery night and the ground was covered in snow. I waited in the woods, keeping an eye on the suspect residence. My portable police radio had an ear piece which allowed for extremely quiet communication.

After some hours in the cold, one of the vehicles from the residence departed. I updated the rest of the crew, who were waiting to surveille the suspect further. One of our guys stayed back and waited several minutes for me to walk back out of the woods. We then headed to join the rest of the guys in tailing the suspect.

That night a search warrant was served at the residence in the woods. It was a substantial house with a substantial quantity of marijuana inside.

THINGS I WISH I LEARNED PRIOR TO UNDERCOVER WORK

Like so many other aspects of law enforcement, the under-cover assignment had a large learning curve. By the time I went back to wearing a uniform, I was just learning tactics that could have been used to catch bigger fish. Just when you're getting more proficient at the job, you're back in uniform.

I had developed contacts within the FBI and DEA, that I did not know prior to that assignment. They had important information and tactics to share. In retrospect, it would have been prudent to assign new UC's to meet and spend some time with these assets.

It also would have been helpful to learn of technology that was accessible and affordable, earlier than I did. Honestly, I was surprised that the team didn't have such tech available when I got there. It would seem that this would be standard equipment for these types of investigative teams. Certainly there's more species of technology which we could have ap-propriated. Granted, advances in gadgetry are increasing exponentially. Still these teams could greatly benefit from additional relevant allocations and semi-regular upgrades.

Years in uniform resulted in me being accustomed to han-dling the entire investigation. After my UC buys resulted in the arrest of suspects, I would generally interview the sub-jects. I should not have. I should have let the other guys do it. There would have been several benefits to having team guys do it. I don't know if it was because I was used to doing all of the investigation on my cases (as when in uniform), my uncertainty about some of the guys' interview abilities, or simply making a foolish decision. There were several guys on the team who would no doubt be able to interview the suspect as proficiently as, or better than I. Some of the newer guys, or guys I didn't know very well, left some question marks for me in this area. Either way I should have probably been taught this. Maybe I was expected to use common sense, and didn't? Whatever the reason was, it should have been explained to me why this was not the best practice. On a few occasions the suspects seemed stunned to see me in the interview room. The bad guys should have been left guessing about who the undercover officers were.

We had a few new guys on the team at around the same time. It felt very much like we were learning on the job. We had some training. But basic training classes at the academy are not as helpful as firsthand experience.

The surveillance training and raid entry training would be exceptions to this; they were solid training courses that were conducted by professionals. MSP ES Team (SWAT) guys who knew what the hell they were doing, so did the surveillance team officers, who had done the job for years.

I think one of the most practical and helpful endeavors could have been a semi-regular gathering with a group of several teams, including guys who were notoriously good at the job even if they no longer did it. This could provide an atmosphere in which new UC's and experienced alike could learn from the successes and mistakes of others. Why perpetually re-invent the wheel?

THE DETERRENCE OF RISK

Illicit narcotics are prevalent everywhere. On numerous different occasions, our team purchased almost every control one substance; marijuana, cocaine, heroin, meth. There was no shortage of the drug problem, and no doubt that we didn't even come close putting a dent in the local supply.

Yet that doesn't mean that the work was pointless. Our society is impacted by the arrests of such people, and addressing the problem at least at some level. It can be compared to the knowledge that officers often catch speeding

116

motorists and issue expensive tickets. This influences many people, including me, to obey the speed limit. People are discouraged from getting behind the wheel after they have been drinking, because of the possibility that they might get arrested. Such an arrest would cause them many problems including; expensive fines, significantly increased insurance premiums, a suspended driver's license, and embarrassment to family and friends. We couldn't catch everyone, but we were busy getting plenty.

The same applies with the drug business. We will not stop all of it; nor could we. Yet we can publicize such cases and put the public on notice, that you might get caught. Police officers provide some level of deterrent.

"It was like a scene from West Side Story, minus the singing and dancing…"

Chapter Eight

OFF DUTY

MR. MOUTH

I was at home watching a Red Wings game. There was a Taco Bell not far from where I lived at the time. During one of the intermissions of the game, I made a run for the border. I wanted to grab some burritos and get back in time to watch the rest of the game. Burritos in hand, I walked out into the parking lot.

As I was walking through the parking lot to my car, some jack-wagon yelled across the lot, "What you looking at bitch?"

He, a buddy, and their girlfriends were walking to their car. I wasn't even walking in their direction, nor they in mine. I guess he was pounding his chest or something, trying to convince a nearby male that he was the alpha dog.

I turned, and started walking towards him. They stopped. It was like a scene from *West Side Story*, minus the singing and dancing. "Hey asshole," I replied, "What you fail to realize is that I'm a state trooper."

"Bullshit," he replied.

I continued towards him and said something like, "We can do this, and I can have about six troopers here in about two minutes if you wanna learn the hard way." He stood looking at me with a curious look, from about twenty feet away. It was close enough that we were able to look each other in the eyes, I got a good look at his face. His look changed from tough guy to inquisitive guy. He returned to his car. Incident averted. I went home, watched the rest of the hockey game, and enjoyed my burritos.

I was relatively young when I graduated from the academy, and the burrito incident happened fairly early in my career. Maybe I didn't look old enough to be a trooper.

Around that time, I even had an old lady ask me for directions at a gas station, while I was in uniform fueling up my patrol car. She then asked me, "Are you even old enough to drive?" I don't know if her statement said more about her or me. Either way I was young.

Anyhow, only providence could have arranged what happened next, not too long after the verbal skirmish at the border. During an afternoon shift, I was driving slowly down the main street of one of the small towns in the post area. The sun was shining, and my window was down, when guess who drove directly passed me in the opposite direction. We both looked each other in the face as we passed.

I quickly turned my patrol car around and stopped him for some traffic violation. We had a brief face to face conversation. He recognized me, and found out that I wasn't bluffing. I checked him through dispatch. What do you know, he had a suspended driver's license.

Handcuffed, vehicle towed away, and a free trip to the jail; the young buck found out his antlers weren't as big as he thought they were. I'm guessing he'll think twice before spouting off at Taco Bell again.

HANGIN' OUT

My dad and I headed over to my buddy's house. He asked for some help moving a washer and dryer into his house and up to the second floor. We moved the appliances, and were having a conversation inside his living room, when we heard

the sound of tires squealing on pavement. We all went outside to check it out.

It wasn't a Mustang or Camaro, but an old blue minivan.
We stood outside for a minute, then the van drove out of
view. A few moments later it drove back onto the same
street, tires squealing as it cornered too fast. It was heading
in our direction from several blocks away.

It was a small neighborhood street, and the speed limit
was probably twenty-five. The van wasn't driving terribly
fast so I wasn't concerned about walking into the street.
The van stopped with me standing in the road. The driver
looked too young to be driving and smelled of alcohol. I
spoke to him through his window and verbally identified
myself as a trooper. My badge and gun were left in my car,
not that it would have helped in this situation.

The young fella got a peculiar look in his eye, and he
stepped on the gas. Old minivans generally don't accelerate
all that fast. I jumped in the window, grabbing the punk in a
headlock with my right arm. I told him to stop, but he kept
driving, while I was hanging out of the window.

I kept squeezing and yelling at him to stop the car. My left
hand grabbed the wheel, both for something to hang onto
and to have some control over the steering. Behind my right
shoulder was a dog in the backseat, it appeared to be a pit
bull or a boxer. I also saw some children in the back seat as
well. "Step on the brake!" I yelled while I pulled on his head
with all of my body weight. I couldn't reach the gear handle
on the right side of the steering wheel.

Meanwhile, my dad ran alongside the van, and jumped
into the open passenger side window. He slammed the vehicle into park. The engine didn't like that, but I did. The
young punk got yanked out of the driver side window by his
head, which I had never let go of. He whined like someone
his age (fifteen). He was now face down on the concrete, I

121

held his hands behind his back as I sat on him, and waited for the city PD to arrive.

My buddy's wife had called the police and they were on scene shortly after I had secured the driver in the middle of the road. The officer got out of his car. The kid complained to him that I wasn't a trooper. The senior officer laughed and said, "Yes he is," as he tossed me his cuffs.

The officer graciously offered to take the report. I advised him that I'd take care of it, and that I could use the overtime anyway. The officer transported the unhappy teenager to his own little jail cell. We got the parents to come to get their children, van, and surprisingly pleasant dog; who happily decided that my shoulder wasn't a chew toy.

I headed to the post, completed the in-custody paper-work, earned some overtime, and headed home with a good story to tell.

Years later my dad and I were having a conversation, probably after watching some military movie, and he said he had always wondered if he would be brave if the situation called for it. I told him that he would, that he had already proved it, and reminded him of the time he jumped into a moving car to save my ass.

24/7

Locking up suspects doesn't mean that you won't encounter them again. I was walking in the mall with a friend who was looking for a ring for his lady. I'm not the mall type and generally prefer to avoid crowded places. As we walked into one of the jewelry stores, I saw him.

He had been arrested for some felony drug charges by yours truly. He looked me in the eyes and clearly recognized me. I told my buddy just in case the SHTF. I was carrying my duty piece, tucked in the waistband of my jeans, and covered by a jacket. I kept an eye on him as he walked out of view. It wasn't the last time I saw him before we left the mall. I went out of my way to make sure he never got behind me.

On another occasion, I was shopping at a local grocery store. While pushing my cart through the aisles I crossed paths with a guy who I had locked up for domestic violence. I knew from a court hearing that the incident/arrest was one of the reasons his wife divorced him.

He recognized me, mean-mugging the whole time. Again, I had my gun tucked under my shirt. I watched him leave the store and drive away before I left. I carried, off duty, every day during my career. Our department actually paid us a small per diem to carry and to be prepared to respond to emergencies.

I tried a half dozen or so holsters. I finally found one that fit my full-size Sig Sauer, and was the most comfortable and practical. What would you know, it was the same one that the thirty-year veteran firearms instructor at the academy had suggested. At the time, I had brushed it off as too simple, and not "Miami Vice" enough. It was a cloth holster, with no strap, and a tough black plastic clip for your waistband or belt. They were durable, although I did wear a small hole through a couple of them after many years of use.

Suspects remember the faces of the officers who locked them up. This is especially so in agencies with smaller patrol areas. Arrests usually take a while and they have plenty of time to get a good look at you.

They know your face. They know what you do. They know how you impacted their lives, and many of them are less than pleased about it. In that sense you are never really off duty.

"once his mouth ran out of ass..."

Chapter Nine

SNOWMAGGEDON

BLIZZARD PROVIDENCE

It was snowing like, well a snow storm in Michigan. Big thick, heavy, wet snow; the kind that makes for disasters on freeways and side roads alike. On days like that most of our shifts were spent helping motorists out of ditches, calling tow trucks for them via dispatch, and providing traffic control until they were safely back on their way.

It didn't take too many shifts during snow storms for slide offs to become events which particularly tried my patience. It became a regular practice to issue the drivers citations for losing control of their vehicles (this was standard procedure for many officers). The drivers would often get upset about this and blame the road conditions. Their anger usually turned to embarrassment when confronted with the fact that numerous cars drove passed us and kept control of their vehicles, while they were waiting to get hauled out of the ditch.

I was dispatched to yet another slide-off, where a 4x4 pickup truck had lost control on the freeway and ended up stuck in the median buried in several feet of snow. This particular slide off happened at a decent curve to the right. My patrol car was parked on the shoulder, on the median side. The driver of the pickup was seated in my front passenger seat. My emergency lights were on, which usually indicates slow down, at least one might think so.

Providentially, it occurred to me that in light of the curve in the highway, that particular point was not the safest place to park. I backed my car up forty to fifty feet or so, hoping to avoid the apex of that curve. It could not have been two or three minutes later that I heard it. Semi-trucks make a distinct sound when sliding across the freeway. I guess that's something you need to experience before you can really appreciate it.

The big rig slid off of the freeway, and into the median, missing the front of my patrol car by just a few feet. It slammed into the median and directly into the pickup truck, dislodging it from the snowy ditch and launching it onto the opposite side of the freeway. The incident was recorded on video (VCR), I kept a copy, but some things like that disappear when you get divorced. It would have easily qualified to be played on COPS, or Real Stories of the Highway Patrol.

After the near-death experience, I pulled my britches out from way up where they didn't belong. I used my high-pitched, 'I almost just died voice' to report it to dispatch. The patrol car was moved to the other side of the freeway, via a nearby turn lane. The semi-truck was entirely in the median, half buried in snow. I trudged through the snow and looked in the window but he was nowhere to be seen. I opened the driver side door and found him lying on the floor behind his seat in the cab area. Apparently, he wasn't wearing his seatbelt and had gotten bounced around a bit, as his truck careened into the ditch and collided with the pickup truck.

As I was checking on the driver, a bob-tail truck (a semi without a trailer hooked up), was visible as it lost control and slid off into the ditch further west of that scene. Minutes later, while I was still on the same scene, a semi with an empty flatbed trailer lost control on the eastbound side of the freeway within eyesight and ended up sideways, blocking all three lanes of traffic.

The truck driver was transported to the hospital for very minor injuries, probably more to be checked out than anything else. I briefly contacted him there to deliver him his excellent driver award. His license was suspended, so he got a few tickets that day. He was still strapped to the transport gurney, conscious and alert. When he saw me, he started crying, I placed the tickets on his chest, and said, "Thanks for not killing me," then walked out.

ANOTHER HAPPY CUSTOMER

On yet another of the familiar nasty snowy days, some jack-wagon ended up in the ditch on a side road. He was pissed off about getting a ticket for losing control of his vehicle on slippery roads. As I turned to head back to the patrol car after delivering his participation ribbon, he got out of his car and squared off at me. He launched a tirade of profanities in my direction, but once his mouth ran out of ass, I asked him, "Are you gonna do something, or are you gonna get in your car and drive away?" Ticket laden and livid, he decided it'd be best to just drive away.

ALMOST GOO

It was the first snow of the year. It came earlier than expected, and my patrol car didn't have snow tires on it yet. You would not believe the difference snow tires make. Apparently, it makes such a qualitative difference that police departments all over the state, including the MSP, swapped out their summer tires for snow tires. The goal was to have this accomplished before the first snow hit. This was quite the task for area tire companies to keep up with.

To say that it was a snowy slippery mess would be an understatement. I had a heck of a time driving up a hill with a fairly slight incline, on a 55-mph highway. My rear tires were spinning more than gripping, and I was getting passed by numerous cars and trucks.

Once I got to the top of the hill, I observed the pickup truck in the ditch on the opposite side of the highway. I turned around, parked as far off the road as possible, and contacted yet another unhappy driver.

We spoke for a few minutes as I explained to him that the law requires drivers to keep their vehicles under control. He whined and moaned about the slippery road conditions. On the one hand he was right, the road conditions sucked. Yes sir, you can have my autograph, let me go get a piece of paper to write it on.

I walked back to the patrol car, opened my door, and heard the unmistakable sound of a vehicle sliding out of control. After years of working in snowmageddons, I had become quite familiar with that sound. I looked back to see a minivan sliding directly at me. My door was open and my options for avoiding this were bad and worse. I didn't even have time to dive into my car, through the open door.

Think thin. I barely had time to jump up onto the frame of the floorboard and hope for the best. I remember watching as the van slid within inches of squishing me, and slammed into the open door of my patrol car. The van then slid into the ditch beyond the truck. I've still got the pictures from that one; the tire tracks through the snow to my damaged patrol car door are clearly visible.

Another trooper responded to handle the accident report involving my car. Imagine our shock upon finding out that the driver of the van had a suspended license. She got an autograph too, just not mine. I was fuming, and avoided speaking to her. She had already won her prize.

A FREQUENT FLYER

The trailer tires of the semi had frozen in place, and the big rig was at a dead stop in the middle lane. The three-lane freeway was a disaster in the category five blizzard. A blend of ice and snow made the road surface as slippery as a greased pig at the county fair.

A local officer had stepped up to help. Many local officers, whose jurisdiction included the freeway, often spent much of their shifts out there during snowstorms. I was not terribly far away from the giant roadblock, while acting as a caution light for some tool who had slid off into the ditch. That day I had to stop often to clear the snow off of the emergency lights of my patrol car.

Dispatch put out a call for a business alarm. The officer behind the semi-truck, warning people not to die, responded to dispatch that it was a frequent flyer alarm. That meant it was an alarm that always went off for no reason. It had zero priority. Even so, the guy who had stepped up, stepped back down, and advised dispatch that he would go and handle the alarm. It was clear to everybody why.

He left the life-threatening scene where there was an 80,000-pound immovable object, in the middle of the freeway, with zero visibility. That officer, would rather go to a nonsense-call than do the real job, and use a patrol car to warn oncoming drivers, in the blinding snow.

I took his place. Any decent officer would have done the same. The reality was that any of us could get hit, on any day. We all know what was at stake. Real police officers put their lives on the line for strangers on a regular basis. This was the job we all signed up to do. That's why we wear body armor, and are armed like soldiers headed into combat. After you've put your life in jeopardy on numerous occasions, and encountered death regularly for other reasons; you come to grips with your own mortality. One of my coworkers told me that every day he drove to work, he thought about the fact that it could be his last shift. He had reached the point where he didn't care, and at least his family would be taken care of. I echoed his words. I had thought I was alone in feeling that way.

My patrol car was parked as far from the semi-truck as it could be, while still lighting up the truck. The spot lights of the patrol car illuminated the reflectors on the top corners of the trailer, and I hoped my emergency lights could be seen through the snow. A giant tow truck eventually arrived and pulled the massive roadblock off of the freeway.

Thankfully, no one died there that day.

DON'T PASS THE PO-PO

Snow tires are amazingly designed, and surprisingly effective. Prior to driving on them, if somebody would have told me that simply changing your tires for the winter would make such a massive difference, I would have called them a liar. I figured it was just another gimmick to prey on those with more cash than common sense.

It was just one more, in a long list of things I've been wrong about. Snow tires, are expletive phenomenal. Patrol car tires were transformed from the equivalent of tennis shoes on an ice rink into near hockey skates.

Don't get me wrong, we couldn't drive seventy-mph on a snowy freeway, but we didn't have to drive twenty-mph either. These tires gripped so much better, sliding around and stopping distance were both significantly decreased. They were indispensable.

Troopers and other officers in Michigan had access to the drive track at the MSP Academy. The track included a 'skid pad.' It was a large, and extremely smooth portion of asphalt (or asphalt type material). This surface would be sprayed with numerous firehose size sprayers.

The patrol cars which would be used on the skid pad had the rear tires exchanged for slick tires, not unlike Nascar

tires. As a driver entered onto the smooth and water covered surface, a driving instructor in the passenger seat
would lock up the rear tires with a button. The car would
begin to slide out of control, as if on icy Michigan roads. The
job of the driver was to regain control of the vehicle, and
avoid a complete spin-out.

While going through the MSP academy, recruits would
each have to master this, along with every other drive track
maneuver. The drive program was intense. All of that to say,
officers in Michigan are well trained to drive in snowy and
icy conditions. Not only were we trained, we gained a ton of
experience as we worked in the wintery weather, for the better part of four months, every year.

So, I was driving on a seventy-mph highway, with two
lanes on each side and separated by a median. Once again,
it was a snowy mess. While I was driving slow enough to
maintain control of my patrol car, with the awesome tires,
traffic began to back up behind me. It's funny, I never ended
up in the ditch while driving in the worst of the wintery road
conditions. I drove for a living, yet everybody still wanted to
pass me.

For many, one plus one didn't equal two, it equaled the
snowy median. One of the poor mathematicians decided she
had enough of driving so slow. I recall the red Camry as it
began to pass me. The woman's car slipped and slid about,
and every additional moment she remained on the highway
was a spin of the roulette wheel.

The Camry didn't have snow tires, nor a professional
driver, nor a math professor at the wheel. As it passed me
more like a sled than a car, I shook my head. The lady in the
red car, had a child in a car seat, in back. Yet apparently, she
had somewhere to be. I could see the handwriting on the
wall and slowed down, letting her pass me.

The concerned mother no sooner passed me, when she
completely lost control of her vehicle. If I hadn't slowed

down, she would have sideswiped my nice new blue car. She fishtailed a bit and then slid off of the roadway and into several feet of snow in the median.

There was an emergency-vehicle-only crossing not too far ahead. I turned around and headed back to check on the bobsled team. While parked on the median side shoulder of the road, I called for a tow truck, to remove yet another car from the ditch. This was money making season for tow companies.

The Camry driver was crying when I contacted her. She and her child were uninjured. Collisions with snow generally didn't result in injuries, except to pride. The lady got a quick math lesson, and learned that it's not a good idea to pass the police on such nasty road conditions.

They say you either write a ticket or give a lecture, but don't do both. She didn't get the entire lecture, but she did get the Cliff Notes version.

"You realize I drive for a living, right?"

"Yes, sir."

"Do you still think it's a good idea to pass a trooper on snowy roads?"

"No, sir."

"I'm glad you're okay. Slow down, and it might be a good idea to invest in snow tires."

Chapter Ten

MULTIFARIOUS

CODE BROWN

I may be breaking a code among law enforcement person-nel by revealing this, but since I no longer wear the blue uniform, I'll share some intel.

When the police drive to emergencies, we call it running code. At least they did in the areas where I worked. Police officers wear a lot of gear. My gun belt was average, and it had to weigh about twenty pounds. There were leather straps with metal snaps which secured the gun belt to a wide leather uniform belt underneath.

Occasionally, nature calls at inconvenient times. Patrol cars are equipped with a lot of things, butt the bumper dumper isn't one of them. There may, or may not have been instances when an officer would use their emergency lights for a personal emergency. If there was such a thing as code brown, it would likely only have been used to get within the vicinity of a facility with some porcelain artwork.

LOGIC & BASIC GEOMETRY

Our MSP dog teams were always on call. However, they needed vacations like the rest of us, and were occasionally out of the area and unavailable. On one-night shift, an of-ficer was in pursuit of a vehicle until it crashed off of the road and into a ditch. The driver beat feet into a thickly wooded area. Several officers checked the area while a local dog team had arrived to go get the bad guy, like a Chesapeake Bay Retriever gets a bird after it's been shot.

Sometimes even birddogs lose the bird. During his track, the municipal officer's dog lost the scent. If you've ever witnessed a dog on a track you could understand why. There's plenty of other scent trails from deer to raccoons and squirrels etc.

Officers stayed in the area for a while, hoping the dog would spook the suspect out from hiding and back into the chase. It may have been an hour or two, but eventually the dog handler called off the track. Officers departed the scene and attended to other responsibilities. My partner at the time was nearing retirement age and wasn't exactly a ball of fire. This trooper didn't hold the reigns very tight and most often handed them to me.

The suspect had originally been seen entering the woods (Point A) to the east. It was quickly determined that the registered owner of the vehicle/possible suspect lived at a residence (Point B) a few miles east of the crash scene. If you were to draw a line from point A to point B, that would be a likely route for the suspect. Not rocket science.

A road ran north and south between Points A and B. There was a small house, situated on this road. The residence was located directly between points A and B.

We moved the patrol car to a small grove of mature pine trees near that residence. There we sat in bat-mobile mode; no lights, in the dark of the nearby pines, with the windows down. My partner was willing to stay in the car, and keep an eye on the road, lest the miscreant should attempt to cross it. I exited the patrol car quietly and watched the tree line, from a position hidden in the pine trees.

It was a nice night, and nothing else was pressing at the time. So we had time to wait. Eventually after we had established the logical trap I watched as the suspect walked slowly out of the woods. The tree line was maybe fifty yards west from my location. Unbeknownst to the suspect, he was headed for the cover of the same grove of pines, where a state trooper awaited his arrival.

The suspect neared to within fifteen or twenty feet. I did my impression of the bad guy in every suspence movie you've ever seen, who jumps out from a hiding place in the dark and sends your popcorn flying all over the place. I scared the piss out of him. The red laser light from my taser probably only added to his state of shock. He gave up instantly. It's plausible that he surrendered more for fear of facing the mosquito mobs again, than me and my taser.

He proceeded to get cuffed and stuffed into my patrol car. Off we drove to deliver the suspect to the original pursuing officer. I was concerned that the guy might need a blood transfusion after all of the mosquitos in the woods had orchestrated a concentrated assault upon his head. Interesting side note, mosquitos have the unique ability to discern between good guys and bad guys. When given the option between the two, the blood-suckers will choose the bad guy every time.

Honestly, I felt bad for the K9 handler that night. I knew him, we worked together often, and he was a likable guy. He had known what had happened because of the police radio traffic.

Sometimes a little information was all that was needed to find the bad guy.

MIND READING

It was on another nightshift when my partner and I answered a dispatched call of a man with a gun, and a possible hostage. Every officer in the area showed up, in this case it was four or five, including us two.

Long guns readied, we made a plan and approached the home with caution. We could see a female on the main level, but no male suspect was in sight. We quickly coaxed her out of the home and moved her away from the scene. After yelling at the suspect for a while we had convinced him to come downstairs and keep his hands up.

A couple of officers had moved in to secure him as fast as possible. The officers laid their long guns on the ground near the door in order to have free hands. I grabbed them and hung them on my shoulder along with mine. The cars were too far away to secure the long guns, and the situation not sufficiently resolved for me to leave the officers with only their side arms. Anyway, I was stuck gun sitting. The thirty-something male subject came out of the house. He was angry, maybe drunk or drugged. For some reason he thought it would be a good idea to walk towards me.

I was about ten or fifteen feet outside of the house near a large tree, with three or four long guns slung over my shoulder. I could see a deputy I knew, closing in behind him.

I had known who the deputy was from high school wrestling. He was a skilled wrestler from a rival school. This guy was a solid 230-250 pounds. At one point later in my career, we were working together in a non-uniform assignment. One of the team guys asked me what I could bench press. I told him 265, I was 200 pounds at the time. He called me on it. Maybe I didn't look like the 265 type. The three of us headed to the department gym. I was hoping I had it in me at the time to put up my max press. I managed one rep of that weight. Then this deputy got on the bench, with the same weight and proceeded to do a dozen or so reps like he was just warming up. The point being, the dude was badass, and not someone you'd want to tangle with.

The suspect continued walking towards me. I could see the deputy behind him. The red dot from my taser was bouncing around on the suspect's chest. The only question was timing. There's a lot of paperwork that comes along with us-

ing a taser, not that I haven't tased my fair share of suspects. But in this case, I didn't think it was going to be necessary, just a plan B. The taser was more of a distraction
than anything.

I didn't say a word to the deputy, nor he to me. The next
second the suspect was inspecting how tall the grass was in
his lawn, from real close like. The deputy dropped the suspect immediately. A stopwatch would have been impressed.
I don't know if I've ever witnessed a suspect being taken to
the ground that fast. The Sheriff himself would have been
proud, but not surprised.

The deputy had done exactly what I expected him to do.
It's kind of funny, at that time the deputy and I had only
worked a few calls together. Yet, because I knew what he
was capable of and what the situation called for; it was clear
to me what he was going to do.

Despite being from different departments, and despite the
animosity which often exists between departments. (Why
the animosity you ask? There's no good reason.) Officers
who arrived on scenes together, knew we were on the same
side seeking the same result.

DON'T INVOLVE THE POLICE

One of the beneficial aspects of the state police to citizens
in Michigan, is that they have the ability to form in large
numbers to deal with crime and violence-plagued areas.
MSP troopers from numerous different worksite locations
were often assigned to these types of details. Most often
such assignments were voluntarily filled. Yet, sometimes it
was not voluntary, as in situations involving large expected
protests, anticipated lawlessness related to out of control
parties, or college and professional sporting events, etc.

My partner and I were assigned to work in an inner-city
area because of increasing problems. It was daylight and we
patrolled the area watching and waiting for trouble. We

would often assist the city police department, as they fielded calls for service. We stopped a vehicle with several occupants for a traffic violation. One by one the subjects consented to a brief search for weapons. Guns were a regular problem there. Gang-related violence and shootings were not infrequent occurrences.

One of the techniques used in such situations, was to have the subject lean on the patrol car, while the officer stood sideways, and placed one foot in-between the subject's feet. This was used in an effort to quickly gain control of a subject, should problems arise, or if the subject would attempt to run. It provided officers with additional reaction time. This was often used in especially troubled areas.

During situations like this, generally one officer acts as back up, while the other goes hands on. My partner was watching from a few feet away. I had one foot between the subject's feet as he leaned against the patrol car.

During the pat down I jarred something loose from the guy's waistband. A handgun fell out of his pants leg onto the ground. When a gun is observed in any situation, officers are trained to yell, "Gun" to inform other officers present. I followed protocol and my partner was instantly assisting me with our body weight pinning the subject to the patrol car. The two of us had no problem securing him in cuffs.

The suspect was in custody for felony CCW (carrying a concealed weapon). The gun was unregistered, this too is illegal in Michigan. Gun control advocates would be up in arms over the fact that he had a gun. Many might believe that more laws are the answer to this problem.

However, the suspect was already disregarding the law. This guy, and thousands of others like him, don't comply with gun laws already in place.

The very nature of law is
that it requires voluntary compliance.

138

We interviewed the arrested individual while on the way to the jail. He stated that he was carrying a gun, because he had already been shot at, and wanted to protect himself. We asked him why not just call the police, report the incident, and let us deal with the shooter(s)?

The suspect said something like, we don't get the police involved. We handle things ourselves. In a great many inner-city areas this mindset is common. In other areas we patrolled (not inner-cities), this wasn't a problem. In fact, citizens outside of such areas are generally glad to get the police involved.

Illegal guns (often stolen), illegally possessed, by law-breaking felons, cause much of the problem relating to gun deaths and injuries. From the vantagepoint of many with boots on the ground, in these war zones, more laws are not the answer to a problem which perpetually involves people already disregarding the law.

In cities such as this one, the hands of the police are often tied, because victims and witnesses are not willing to talk to cops. This perspective only perpetuates the problems.

PINK

The weather was cool and enjoyable on yet another night shift. We were dispatched to a suspicious vehicle parked down the street from a residential area. The peculiar location of the vehicle indicated that somebody was out there and up to no good. My senior partner was driving. He turned the headlights off, a simple practice which had proven helpful in catching many nocturnal miscreants. He drove slowly, windows down, listening. I was the junior trooper in the car, and he directed me to go out on foot while he continued in the patrol car.

A dog barking in the middle of the night is often helpful in locating trouble makers. I headed in the direction of the agitated K9. Walking slowly and quietly through back yards I listened and searched using my flashlight for quick checks.

My flashlight beam crossed something out of place. I directed the light towards the object, and I was rather surprised to see a young man sitting quietly on a back porch staring at me. He had pink spiked hair and a black collar around his neck with silvery studs. He had an unusual, deer in the headlights look on his face. It was clear that he wasn't supposed to be there. I advised my partner via radio, and shined my light in the air so he could find me. While waiting for my partner, I asked the strange fellow a few questions. I asked if he was out here alone, he replied that he wasn't. I asked him who he was with and where. Pinky pointed to an area behind me, and said there was a girl on a red bike.

There was no girl or red bike anywhere within sight. This was the first time I had encountered somebody who was hallucinating. It's rather eerie. My partner arrived and we secured the subject in cuffs. The suspicious car was his.

Needless to say, a person who's seeing things that are not there is not a reliable source of information. We headed to his house to contact family members and get some sort of helpful info. My partner exited the car and pounded on the front door. I sat with the delusional gent. He asked me to turn the music off. The radio wasn't playing. He asked why we were there.

I told him we were looking for his parents, and he said his mom was right there standing outside at my car door. She wasn't. Why I looked, I couldn't tell you. It was freakish, like an X-Files episode.

Nobody was home so we took the subject to the hospital. We babysat while the medical staff did what they do. Hours later, when the guy was finally able to have a coherent conversation, he admitted that he took a whole package of pseudo-ephedrine.

Here I had just thought he had used too much hair dye.

DEERANGED

Deer are plentiful pretty much everywhere in Michigan. That is except Hockey-Town, otherwise known as D-town, the Big D, or the war zone. Anyway, car vs. deer accidents were among the more regular calls we were dispatched to. I probably spent most of my career dealing with drunks, domestics, deer, deplorable thieves, drug users and dealers; likely in that order. Today, we're gonna learn about the letter D.

One wintery night shift, my partner and I were headed out of the city, and into rural-land. He was driving. We had barely even reached the city limits when a deer decided he'd run next to us, parallel. My partner slowed down, so did the dauntless deer, who then decided he wanted to see whose antlers were bigger and charged the patrol car. The buck's head and antlers were hit by our windshield, and his body slammed against the driver side door, shattering the window.

My partner had glass all over him. The deer realized he should move on to smaller bucks. He was apparently unfazed by the collision and ran off into the snow. The glass covered driver pulled the car over. I couldn't help but laugh, but he was pissed.

"Get the long guns, let's get that bastard!" he said.

We may or may not have attempted to track the deer through the snow. Whether we did or not, the big buck had escaped, no doubt on his way to get a cold one and some ibuprofen.

SHOWING OFF

On one of the days during the FTO program (Field Training Officer), my regular training officer was unavailable, so I was assigned to work with another trooper for the day. We were dispatched to a car vs. deer accident. Often the deer was injured; with broken legs, or otherwise unable to move. Putting the injured deer out of its misery, was a regular part of handling car/deer crashes. That was the case on this occasion.

Previously I had heard stories about officers getting irritated that their duty 9mm pistol didn't have enough ass to put down an injured deer. Often, they had to shoot the deer numerous times. Having had the inside scoop, I was about to impress my training officer of the day. I'd break out the .357 Magnum; that'll to do the trick.

A farmer came out to visit the troopers in front of his house and check out the injured deer. Many people would take a deer that had been killed by a car, and turn it into steaks for the dinner table. Some people even put their names on a list at dispatch to request any deer that were killed by cars which hadn't been claimed.

The well-respected trooper, and the farmer stood not too far away as I was about to put the injured animal down. I took careful aim at the deer's melon. Kablaaam! The Magnum round was sent down range and directly into the deer's head, which recoiled from the impact. I waited a bit, surely that had to work. The deer made a sound which only injured deer make, and stared at me. Kablaaam! The second shot had the same effect. My ears were still ringing from the first shot, and now doubly so. The T-1,000 deer was still staring at me.

This isn't going well I thought. Anybody ought to be able to put down a wounded deer with dos grande bulletos. Not me, not that day. Three strikes and you're out, I had one more at bat. As you might expect the third shot had the same result.

142

I was hitting the deer in the head. This was clear even to my two increasingly unimpressed witnesses, as the deer's head wobbled with each impact. My ears were ringing like a fire alarm at the local firehouse.

Five .357 rounds and the deer finally entered the pearly gates. We all got to enjoy hours of ringing ears. Apparently, deer have fairly small brains in their large heads. I was never a hunter, plus I missed deer anatomy day in high school. My training officer thanked me for contributing significantly to his hearing loss. I didn't receive high marks that day. The story spread around the post, and I learned to shoot deer in the heart not the head.

I added my share of experiences to the ever-growing list of reasons why the new guys are called cubs.

THE MOUSE

My midnight shift partner and I were dispatched to a fight in progress. It was in a rural area, at a small farm. We arrived to find several edgy subjects. They indicated that an intoxicated male was causing the problem.

We confronted him in front of a large garage. Each of us slowly approached from a different forty-five-degree angle, the three of us forming a triangle. The thirty-something white male looked at each of us, like a mouse trapped between two advancing cats.

He shifted his gaze from one of us to the other. The mouse split and dashed around the corner of the garage. You wouldn't think that such a situation would be humorous, but this one was. There were two of us, and he was drunk. I laughed as we began our foot pursuit. I recall several occasions when someone fled on foot, that I laughed. Maybe it was a nervous laugh, or maybe it was because I knew that particular individual was only delaying the inevitable. There were however several that pursuits that did not involve me laughing.

143

The suspect made it around the second corner, with my partner and I hot on his tail. He darted behind a stack of pallets behind the building. My partner followed. I chose the intercept location not far away, to the only place the suspect could exit. I readied my taser. The drunken speedster was either gonna get introduced to my size twelve boot in his chest, or the power-packed voltage of the taser; whichever was most prudent. My partner flushed him out. As the suspect fled from my partner, he unknowingly ran headlong in my direction. From fairly close range I pulled the trigger. The loud pop of the taser cartridge exploded, as it blasted the two probes out from the device and firmly into the suspect's chest.

A collision with my boot was unnecessary. He dropped in his tracks. The electricity surged along his torso, in a direct line between each of the two small barbs. The taser did exactly what it was designed to do.

Tasers have saved countless lives, as police officers have been provided with a less-lethal option for dealing with combative subjects. Death is an extremely rare occurrence with these devices. It is rare enough that when it does happen, it usually makes the national news.

ASSAULT WITH A GOLF CLUB

On a chilly night shift, I had a different partner than usual; it was probably a holiday. He was one of the most senior guys at the post, who had always worked the day shift. Like a lot of guys, he wasn't about to turn down holiday pay, even if it meant working a night shift. This trooper was about as nice as they come. He had a master's degree in something; but it was evidence that sometimes a degree is just a piece of paper. The gentle, happy trooper would barely qualify as a butter-knife in a drawer full of steak-knives. Needless to say, that didn't exactly motivate me to pursue higher education. Not that I didn't, but that was years later.

There were only a few occasions on which I worked with trooper Happy. This one included him driving to a local donut shop. I was less than pleased about his choice excursion. I told him, "I'll just wait in the car."

He replied, "No you won't. You're coming with me."

When a senior trooper gives you reasonable directions, you listen, otherwise there may be unnecessary trouble. Preferring to avoid trouble, I listened to my senior officer and we walked into the Casa-de-Donuts. He walked up to the restaurant bar and took a seat. It was humiliating. I took a seat next to him. Señor Donut ordered a cup of coffee and a donut. A glass of water was ordered by the junior trooper. It was a good thing this was before the proliferation of smart phones. Officer Happy and I would have been plastered all over the internet; memes galore.

My highly educated partner and I responded to assist a local officer at the scene of an AWDW (assault with a deadly weapon). Upon arrival it was extremely evident that there had indeed been an assault, and somebody was seriously injured. A stream of blood was flowing in the street, down a slight decline away from the scene. I was surprised at the volume of blood.

The male victim had been severely beaten with a golf club. Once the two suspects had broken the nine iron, they began to stab him with the shaft of the club. The suspects were long gone before the police arrived. My partner commented that it looked like a scene from a horror movie. I wasn't a horror-flic buff, so maybe he was right but it was definitely a bloody mess.

We remained at the scene until the paramedics arrived and hauled the victim away to the hospital. The victim lived, but I'm guessing it was due to a few units of blood donated by some generous citizen(s).

NO STRINGS ATTACHED

The son of a friend of mine, did one of his first police ride-alongs with me. Later he worked for a small department in an area I covered. He eventually got accepted into the MSP Academy. By this time, he was much taller than I and significantly more muscular. He had good genes. Me, not so much.

Sunday afternoon through Friday evening, recruits were getting pummeled at the academy. I'd call him on the weekends and encourage him to stick it out and that it would be worth it at the end.

One of those weekends, he told me that he had enough and he wasn't going back.

I told him, "Bullshit you're not going back. I'll beat your ass."

After the following night shift I drove my Honda VFR rocket to his house. It was usually a ninety-minute trip. For some reason, that morning the trip didn't take that long.

I confronted my worn-out buddy in his back yard. He dwarfed me, yet I told him, "I'll beat your ass right here if you quit. You're going back." I meant it.

I also spoke to his wife, and encouraged her to motivate him to fight through till the end. He ended up back at the academy that Sunday.

Some conversations are exceptionally productive. That one with him, in his backyard, was one of those. Another came when I spoke to my boss about him. I told the boss that this guy wouldn't cause him any headaches and would be a hard charger. Post Commanders had some pull with the academy in regards to where new troopers would get assigned. I didn't have the strings to pull, but my boss did. Of all of the places to get assigned across the entire state of Michigan, guess where my buddy ended up working.

When he graduated from the academy, he had lost a lot of weight due to all the running, but afterwards he ballooned

146

up to his previous NFL linebacker size. He was enormous. I have a picture of both of us standing side by side, in uniform. I looked like a kid by comparison.

AIDS

I responded to assist an officer with a fight, and it was the officer who called for assistance, rather than dispatch. That gets your heart pumping, knowing that a fellow officer is urgently calling for help. I pushed the patrol car hard and was there within a few minutes.

The township officer worked in an area just outside of the city limits, with a population of several hundred thousand. I arrived in the rough neighborhood, and parked in front of the trailer next to the officer's car. I could hear the commotion coming from inside the trailer.

The officer was visible inside, physically struggling with a bloody subject. I ran into the melee. This was before we had access to tasers. So, it was fisticuffs. As we attempted to subdue the bloody man, he kept yelling, "I have AIDS." That's not happy news when your job is to secure a combative blood covered man by physical means.

The two of us drove the suspect to the ground and secured him in cuffs. We were a bloody mess afterwards. The officer transported the subject to the jail via the cage in his rear seat. I called the Sergeant and explained that I was covered with the blood of a guy who repeatedly said he had AIDS.

I ended up waiting in the E.R., while my boss and the medical staff tried to come up with a game plan for how to deal with this. I was facing the option of taking a toxic cocktail of meds. That option wasn't something I wanted to volunteer for, yet I also didn't want to get AIDS. The scales tipped heavily in the direction of the vexatious medication medley. We waited for a while.

It was reassuring that my boss was no fool. He was a bad-ass. He could do pull-ups for days and outrun all of us during annual physical training evaluations. He was as capable intellectually as he was physically. This supervisor was a nice guy, but could also kick your butt when necessary. We all respected him.

Eventually it was determined that the suspect did not have the disease, and thankfully I got to avoid the wicked meds.

"Hi honey, I'm home. How was your day?"

"Well I tangled with a bloody guy, and thought I was exposed to AIDS. I narrowly avoided a nasty concoction of medicine. Turns out the guy didn't have AIDS, and I didn't have to take the meds."

I had been playing my Beatles record, sitting on the living room chair in my underwear, and plucking on the strings of my guitar. At least that was how I had learned to deal with stressful situations, a lesson I picked up from Nicholas Cage.[5]

POOR DRIVERS

It's a common saying, in America, that people do not know how to drive. In many cases this is no exaggeration. My favorite is the uber-expertise of some who drive in serious weather conditions. I wish I knew the number of people who I had dealt with whose excellent driving skills had launched them off of the road and into ditches, medians, guard rails, and so on. In the nasty Michigan winter weather, ten or more in a day would not be unusual. If I handled one hundred per year for my career, well over one thousand would be fairly plausible. The simple act of reasonably reducing speed could have prevented a great majority of those.

---

[5] Director Michael Bay, *The Rock*, 1996

One lady who probably took drivers education on several occasions, was driving on a snowy freeway. Eventually she decided that the road conditions were too poor to drive on. She tried to turn around in at least a foot of snow on the shoulder. As a result her car had become uniquely buried in the snowy mess. She didn't want to be like everybody else and drive a few miles up to the next exit ramp to return home. She was a trailblazer, or at least she wanted to be.

Police officers regularly deal with those among us with poor driving abilities. Imagine my frustration, when I had initiated a traffic stop, and the driver decided to stop in the fast lane of a seventy-mph freeway. I rushed up to her driver side window and told her to drive onto the shoulder on the median side. To my surprise the lady actually had a valid driver's license.

Near the top of my list of excellent driving skills, is failing to move over for emergency response vehicles. These non-mover-overs were oblivious to all the bright flashing lights and blaring sirens behind them. One of the most frustrating things about these drivers, was that we could not stop them and issue tickets, because we were urgently needed else-where.

Another problem which occasionally causes fatalities, is failing to move over for emergency personnel when they are stopped on the side of the road. Many police officers have been killed because someone didn't move into the second lane. The simple act of slowing down when an officer is seen on a traffic stop and driving over into the next lane, could save lives. In many states there are move over laws which require motorists to do just that. In Michigan there was a hefty fine for disregarding this law.

It must be also be common misconception that the speed limit is merely a suggestion. I could have written speeding tickets all day every day. In fact, I know one trooper who did. At one of my post assignments, a guy who was the most senior trooper at the post always worked freeway traffic. There was a traffic assignment position on the schedule and his name was always on it. The man was a machine; day in and day out he would write an average of fifteen tickets per shift (that's moving). Fifteen tickets in an eight-hour shift (minus a thirty-minute lunch break and fifteen minutes starting and ending your shift) is an average of one ticket issued every twenty-eight minutes. Each traffic stop could easily take fifteen minutes. That leaves about fifteen minutes to go fishing for the next one. For as long as I worked with him, he did that every day. I moved to a different post, but as far as I know, he continued his ticket writing frenzy until he retired.

Many motorists neglect two simple actions which could reduce the number of vehicle crashes significantly: increasing following distance, and obeying speed limits. It has been said that a following distance of one car length for every ten-mph is appropriate. It should probably be more. More room in front of you results more time to react to potential problems. After seeing no shortage of serious traffic crashes, I make a habit of keeping a significant following distance from vehicles ahead.

Speed limits exist for a reason. That said, just because the sign says seventy-mph doesn't mean you should drive that fast in the snow or rain. Good drivers reduce their speed during poor weather conditions.

I realize that this is common sense advice. The problem is that a multitude of drivers simply do not use common sense.

Chapter Eleven

LESSONS LEARNED

ANOMALIES

General Mad Dog Mattis, wrote an endorsement for the book *Left of Bang*, which was written by two commanding officers in the United States Marine Corps. In their book, they analyze the subject of human behavior and survey the concept of intuition, as it relates to the military. The primary purpose of their project is to train soldiers to recognize a particular set of human behaviors for the purpose of what they call combat profiling. The Marine Commanders describe a normal level of behavior as, "baseline" and unusual patterns of human behavior as, "anomalies."[6] The book is dedicated to the issue of preemptive, active observation. The goal is to prevent disaster before it happens. The authors highlighted and examined several "Universal Human Behaviors" to help identify these anomalies.

One of their stories is the account of an airport police officer, who acted on her instincts, and interdicted a large quantity of explosive materials.[7] She couldn't put her finger on it, but something felt wrong. It was as if her subconscious had noticed small details that she wasn't consciously perceiving. The little officer on her shoulder was jumping

---

[6] Van Horne and Riley, Left of Bang, p. 53
[7] Ibid. p. 65

up and down, trying to get her attention. She listened to her instincts, and investigated further. If the officer had disregarded her intuition, the suspect would have gone unnoticed, and crowds of people could have been killed or injured.

Paying attention to details, and instincts can save lives, including your own.

ANOMALIES PART II: IT JUST SEEMED WRONG

One of my mentors described an incident that didn't really make sense to me, until he showed me the video. He was on a traffic stop, on the shoulder of a major highway. There were two male subjects in the car. The trooper had one subject out and spoke with him.

At one point both subjects from the car were outside when one of the guys turned his head sideways and spit, within view of his compadre. The trooper recognized that something was wrong. The way he spit was wrong; he wasn't just clearing his throat. The trooper trusted his instincts, he backed up and quickly escalated to the top of the food chain. My friend knew that circumstances can go from zero to sixty in seconds. He could too.

The two men backed down when faced with the trooper's quick and potent response. When we watched the video, I could see the small detail that he had picked up on. The two men were facing the trooper and one of them communicated to the other, let's do this. If my mentor wasn't paying attention to detail, he might not be here today.

Call it intuition, a gut feeling, a sixth sense, the little guy on your shoulder, or divine intervention; it doesn't matter how you label it, just listen.

ANOMALIES PART III: SOMETHING INSIDE ME KNEW

In the first chapter of this book, under the heading *SCHWACK!!!*, I described an incident where anomalies were way outside of the baseline. The small details were the look in the man's eyes, the tone of his voice, and the way he said, "After you." This was atypical behavior. Usually, even on the scene of a domestic violence incident, people comply with being separated, interviewed, and occasionally detained in handcuffs.

The subject's initial behaviors alone would have been enough to raise my level of officer action. However, these weren't the only indicators that something was wrong: I was there on a call of domestic violence, the man verbally refused direction from me, and then used physical force to prevent my efforts to simply detain him. All of this was screaming at me that something was wrong. I recognized the anomalies, and officer action escalated as a result.

Being too laid-back in this job, can result in a long funeral procession. There is a reason the MSP academy beat it into our heads to pay attention to detail. When the small red flags start waving in the wind, it's time to act.

ANOMALIES PART IV: NORMAL HUMAN BEHAVIOR

In the previous chapter on Traffic Patrol, under the headings of *Subconscious Physical Reaction to External Stimuli*, and *He Won't Notice*, I highlighted examples of some anomalies. Motorists usually react to the presence of a patrol car, in a normal and predictable manner. When a person's actions are well out of the range of ordinary, it's a strong indication that something is wrong.

WATCH THEIR HANDS

I don't recall who first told me the phrase, "Watch their hands, it's their hands that can kill you." It seems like obvious advice but it's worth a closer look. Action is faster than reaction. Therefore, getting a head start by keeping their hands in view, just might save your life.

One of my best friends is a veteran police officer; he's the kind of friend you have for life. He experienced this lesson up close and in person. He had just made contact with a potential suspect. In the brief moment of contact, a portion of the suspect's body was behind a door. In the next second the officer was shot with a gun at point blank range, near his face.

My friend was shot with a pistol, he never saw it until it was fired. The officer returned fire, and killed the suspect. Thankfully my friend's injury was not life threatening. However, it did sideline him for a while. He would tell you the exact same thing, "Watch their hands. It's their hands that can kill you."

The Marine authors highlight the importance of this lesson, as well as that of observing a subject's attention:

> *The first area of the body Marines should observe on a person is the hands. Checking the hands of a person ensured that the person is not holding a weapon and is not preparing to strike. Marines should ensure that any person they come into contact with exposes his or her hands - this will help to ensure the person is not an immediate threat. Making the decision to contact a person often involves getting physically close and creates a significant amount of risk: limited reaction time, increased number of options for the attacker to do harm, and less skill required by an attacker to do harm...*

Another indicator to look for is people who are "checking their six." This is when a person looks over the shoulder to see who is around or behind them. Only people who are aware of their surroundings conduct this behavior, and since most people do not bother to search for threats or bother to be aware of their surroundings, this is an indicator that demands further observation. As discussed earlier, people are categorized into one of three categories: Good guys, bad guys, and the rest of the population. Good guys (Marines, soldiers, police officers, etc.) are trained to be aware of their surroundings and will conduct this act of checking their six to see if anyone is approaching them, to look at the people around them and to maintain a general level of awareness. Bad guys (criminals, insurgents, terrorists, etc.) will conduct the same type of behavior to assess the area for easy targets and to ensure there are no "good guys" around them who could catch them in the act. Any person checking his or her "six" is immediately an anomaly and deserves further observation.[8]

HANDS UP

Our team had planned the deal in detail. It was going to be a buy/bust with a suspect who had already committed several felonies, and was about to commit more. The plan included me, not identifying myself as a police officer. I was a UC so my job was to do the deal, say the magic words, and then distract the suspect until the team snagged him up.

As anyone in the military will tell you, things often don't go as planned. Well as you might imagine, our plan didn't work out exactly as we had designed it.

---

[8] Van Horne and Riley, *Left of Bang*, p.88-89

The suspect and I met at the pre-arranged location. We were in a large parking lot. I was backed in to a good spot, and I could see some team members. The bad guy sat in my car, and sold me his product. Once the deal was done, I dropped the signal phrase, and waited for the guys to sweep in. They were already nearby, and started moving in our direction.

I could see a deputy rapidly approaching my vehicle from the front. His gun was drawn and he was clearly marked with the unmistakable yellow word, "SHERIFF" on his chest. The deputy was quickly moving out from the parking spaces across from me. I could see some others moving out the corner of my eye, but my focus was on the suspect in my passenger seat. I could clearly see his left hand, but his right hand had slipped out of my view and down by his right leg.

It was at that second that I ordered him, with an intense tone, "Put your hands up." He looked at me sideways. I said it again louder, "Put your fucking hands up I'm the Pohleece." Both of his hands sprung up in the air, empty. He was promptly removed from the car. Whether he wanted to go or not was irrelevant.

Later during a debrief on the situation, I was reprimanded by a supervisor who had never once done the job that I was doing. He screamed at me about violating our arrangement, by identifying myself as a cop, and putting others in jeopardy because of it. I explained my case to no avail. I had acted out of instinct on a split-second decision.

I got written up for disregarding orders or something like that. My file was clean, and I was pissed. The whole incident had been recorded on video. I watched the video a few times and noted the time between me telling the suspect to put his hands up and identifying myself as a police officer. It was four seconds from the time those words came out of my mouth until the suspect was being ripped out of the vehicle. There wasn't even time to endanger anyone.

At the discipline hearing, I advised that I had video of the incident. The hearing officers were surprised to see that I had brought the video. They could count the seconds themselves. Of those seated across the table from me, one had worked in my position and/or closely supervised people who did. After watching the video, no deliberation was needed. That paper tiger ended up as a trophy mounted on my wall. Rumor has it that copies of that video are still around, somewhere.

TACTICAL TECHNOLOGY

During my career only two officers, that I was aware of, had night vision monoculars. They had purchased them on their own. Thermal optics were much more expensive then, and the only places I had encountered them were at a few fire departments.

Night vision and thermal vision would have proven helpful during incidents that involved searching for suspects, or lost Alzheimer patients. There is no doubt that both of these widely available options could result in lives saved.

Now, it seems that every officer either has, or should have, a body cam. People lie. An officer would be well served by having evidence to defend himself or herself from false accusations. There were a number of false accusations made against officers, of sexual assaults or otherwise. Many of which were able to be proven false by patrol car dash cams. During most of my career we either had no 'in car camera,' or when we began to, we only had them in some of the patrol cars. Eventually they became more prevalent and had finally evolved from a VCR in the trunk to digital video.

Rifle optics were only ever seen on SWAT team level weapons, at least in the MSP. Yet in many agencies, officers can purchase their own rifles and optics. If the SHTF would you prefer access to a rifle with or without optics?

BRAKE FADE

It's one thing to hear the term brake fade, it's something entirely different to experience it. The only times that I encountered the effect were during vehicle pursuits. Occasionally it was an extended period of time before a suspect could be stopped, whether by stop-sticks, patrol car intervention, or otherwise.

The first time I was introduced to the vehicle debilitating condition was when a fellow officer had initiated a traffic stop, but the suspect wanted to race. Numerous patrol vehicles joined in the pursuit. That's generally a violation of written policy, but as is the case with so many other situations; it's better to be judged by twelve than carried by six. We weren't going to let another officer face the dangerous situation alone.

Full acceleration, the engine roars, and the patrol car launches like a crotch-rocket. At least the Dodge Chargers did. They were the meanest version of patrol car that I had ever driven. Pursuits also involve rapid braking, whether it's for turns, crazy traffic, or other patrol cars.

I was flying to assist the lead car, and I wasn't the only one. Another patrol car was coming from the opposite direction as me, we were both gonna make the turn. Unexpectedly the other officer turned in front of me. I slammed on the brakes, but they didn't respond the way I was used to; with a rapid deceleration.

It was like all of the sudden I had the brakes of a Toyota Prius. My angry car engine wanted to go, and my brakes had given up. I was standing on the petal, and my car stopped just in time to avoid hitting the other police vehicle. My surprisingly spongy brakes almost caused a collision with another patrol car. His car made the turn before me, and I followed. A short while later the suspect crashed in a construction mess, and took off on foot. He wasn't as fast as he thought he was.

That was one of the longer pursuits I had been involved in. The intense stop and go driving caused the brakes to get so heated up that it drastically impacted the stopping distance. Had they worked like they always did, like I expected them to; it wouldn't have been so close to a disaster. The car does have an excellent braking system, one of the best, if not the best I've ever used. Yet even the best start to struggle during such extended periods of heat and stress. This effect can happen when you least expect it.

The expert drivers at the MSP academy taught us to drive at eighty-percent of our ability, even in emergency situations. They repeatedly verbalized this lesson; save yourself that extra twenty-percent for the just in case circumstances, leave yourself and your car some ability to react when the unexpected happens. Many officers die in vehicle crashes, often while in the course of emergency driving. It was ingrained in our minds, that if you drive at one-hundred-percent of your ability, you have nothing left for the unforeseen. Officers are regularly informed of stories involving other officers losing control of their vehicles. Pushing a patrol car too hard can prove disastrous, and I nearly found out the hard way.

PEPPERONYA

A local officer had gone to an apartment, seeking to locate and arrest a suspect. My partner and I went to assist. The nature of the incident was such that it was prudent to bring additional officers as back up.

The three of us approached the apartment building in the dark and entered the hallway. The originating officer knocked on the door, and a female subject opened it to greet us. Harboring a fugitive is a crime. Simply informing residents of this generally results in an open door. She advised that the suspect was present inside. We entered into the small two-bedroom apartment.

159

The suspect was cornered, but he wasn't interested in going anywhere. Typically, people voluntarily surrender to the handcuffing process. But this was not a usual situation. Red flags were flapping in the wind, as the suspect faced three officers and didn't back down. This definitely fit into the anomaly category.

We weren't about to wait around to see if he had a reason for his actions, like a weapon or otherwise. Three officers recognized the unusual behavior, and launched into subdue mode. The suspect was pummeled to the ground as each of us played a role in the coordinated effort. As in so many other situations, we learned to rapidly triage a situation to determine what action is needed and where.

We didn't need to speak to each other. This wasn't our first rodeo clown. The suspect still presumed it was a good idea to resist, even as he was on the floor with the three of us on top of him. I was becoming increasingly pissed off. Officers are not immune to injury, and I had my fill of this guy's resistance.

Wanting to end the scuffle sooner, I reached for my pepper spray: which was a potent combination of CS (Orthochlorobenzalmalononitrile), and OC (Oleoresin Capsicum). This is basically a concoction of tear gas (which significantly irritates the respiratory system), and an intense substance derived from extremely hot peppers (this causes a powerful, but temporary burning sensation to the skin).

One of the officers said, "No! Don't spray it in here!"

The warning was a second too late, the suspect had already gotten a face-full. He was instantly miserable. We also began to feel the lung burning effects of the spray. The suspect instantly gave up, was cuffed, and brought out of the apartment. We expedited the process on account of my excellent decision, which left us all coughing and gagging. My fellow officers were not impressed. Once we were outside the effects on us began to dissipate in the fresh air.

The apartment complex sprinkler system was on, and the grass was soaked. The subject in cuffs begged me to let him put his face in the water of the sprinkler. Since I was the one who sprayed him, I let him. There was no need to leave him with the burning substance all over his face.

The suffering combatant laid in the wet grass, and put his face as close to the sprinkler as possible. While I know the effects of the spray are extremely unpleasant, the sight was laughable. Maybe next time he won't fight with the police.

It seems like a universal experience for officers, that at some point they end up getting sprayed from another officer's pepper spray. I've been in a few of those situations, either close by, down-wind, or both. Sometimes we'd catch some of the over spray. None of this bodes well for making friends.

Once subjects who have been sprayed are subdued and in cuffs, it is protocol to attend to them and try to help wash/wipe the spray from their face. This is generally done by officers on scene or paramedics or jail personnel.

The morals of the story: Don't use pepper spray in confined areas, and don't fight with the poh-leece.

RACISM

There was one African-American trooper who I worked with often. I hate that phrase, because he's an American. Period. The worst racism that I have ever witnessed, was African-Americans maliciously slandering African-American officers. Apparently, in some segments of our country it is detestable for an African-American to become a police officer.

Nobody calls me a Caucasian American, nobody calls white people European Americans, Norwegian Americans, or Irish Americans. At least not in any seriously derogatory manner that I am aware of. How is it that in the twenty-first century humanity is still concerned with skin color?

161

Anyway, this trooper is one of the best human beings I know. He is brave, hard-working, he is superior to me intellectually and physically. He's a dad, a husband, and a Michigan state trooper in the truest sense. When he shows up on your doorstep, you know that you just encountered the real deal. He is solid gold.

We were night shift partners on numerous different rotations. I enjoyed the hell out of working with him. Night shift sucks if you're stuck with a partner that you don't like. That wasn't the case with him, he was one of my favorite people to work with.

One of the funny aspects of the night shifts we worked together was the driver gets to rule the radio. This was a fairly common rule among night shifters. We alternated drivers every other shift. He would turn on the jazz station, or if he was in the right mood, rap, or other music I wasn't familiar with. I didn't mind, it was broadening my horizons. When I drove, it was usually country music and he didn't mind.

On one particular shift we had backed up a city officer on a call. I have never been spoken to like my partner was that night (and it wasn't the only time). Several African-American people (I genuinely don't know if there's a better phrase, if there is, imagine I'm using that one) that we encountered unleashed on him verbally. I won't repeat what was said to him on that occasion in my presence, but it's the most offensive way I have ever heard anyone speak to a police officer.

The tirade was solely based on his skin color. This was intense racism. It was hatred. On several such occasions I'd get pissed off and step up to tell somebody what time it was. But my partner would calmly restrain me, and deal with them in a professional manner. He'd say something like, "I got this." or "Let me deal with this." I listened to him, not just because he was senior to me, but because I respected him too much to do otherwise.

162

In many inner-city areas police officers are despised. In these areas, from what I witnessed, African-American police officers are abominated by many people of the same race. They are viewed as traitors, though they are precisely the opposite.

As far as racism in law enforcement, the MSP took a serious stance on the issue. We had mandatory trainings regarding racism and race matters in our day. Our daily reports recorded the race of everyone contacted during traffic stops. We had African-Americans in command officer positions and an African-American served as director of the Michigan State Police for several years. I guess I didn't see racism as a major issue either in the MSP or otherwise. It was not lost on me that our country had elected an African-American president. That election has provided some much-needed perspective for America on the issue of racism in our day, or perhaps it should.

The use of fatal force by police officers is a hot-button issue in our day, especially in regards to minorities. The fact is that more Caucasian people are fatally shot annually by law enforcement officers than otherwise. Without a doubt I will not be the first nor last to highlight the fact that there is an unbalance in media coverage of police shootings. If a Caucasian American is shot by police the incident barely qualifies as a newspaper story. Why is it different otherwise?

As far as my career goes, my assigned post areas included *numerous* cities which were largely populated by minorities. Of the nine uses of fatal force by police officers who I personally knew and worked with, seven of the subjects killed were Caucasian (six males and one female) and two were African-American males. All of which were investigated and declared justified uses of fatal force.

From a law enforcement perspective, one statistic that so often seems to be left out of the fatal force discussion and race is the number of officers murdered annually. According to the FBI, in 2018 alone, fifty-five police officers were murdered.

Why is race not an issue when a cop is shot? Because it's not a matter of race, it's a matter of humanity, or the lack thereof.

TRUST NO ONE

Before I became a police officer, a trooper who was a good friend, told me not to become a cop. He said I would become grumpy, and cynical like him. That didn't seem too bad, I liked him well enough. I respected the work he did. He was an ass-kicker, and proved it repeatedly. He set the bar. I spent my career trying to catch up to him. He was right, like he was about a lot of things. I'm about as cynical as it gets.

Police work quickly provided countless incidents which revealed how many people in our world lie, and how frequently. They will lie about not wearing their seatbelt, speeding, about stealing and cheating. Even when you've caught them red handed, or shoe printed, or when there's phone marks on faces. People lie about their names, even though they can't spell the fake ones and their date of birth, when they can't do basic math. A country song splains it well:

> *"You lie like the man with slicked back hair, who sold me that Ford. You lie like a pine tree in the back yard after last month's storm. You lie like a penny in the parking lot at the grocery store. It comes way too natural to you... well it's what you do, it's who you are."* [9]

One of the most difficult lessons I had to learn, is more about humanity, than police work. I cannot list all of the

---

[9] The Band Perry, *"You lie"*

stories of betrayal that I witnessed. If I did, this project might never get finished.

There are some supervisors who only have the goal of climbing the ladder. They will step on anyone in their way to do so. Many will target officers of lower rank, seeking to discipline them; so that they might show the ability to do the "difficult" work of supervising. Many officers have been betrayed by people who were once coworkers who became supervisors. These turncoats exchanged their shiny silver badges for tarnished ones.

Some officers will turn on another in the same rank and at the same department. Guys who are supposed to be able to trust each other can become as unprincipled as the criminals we locked up. Imagine being on a domestic, in the middle of the night, in a rough neighborhood, and having to keep as much of an eye on the other officer as you do on the suspects. Now, don't imagine it because it happens.

I know several, solid gold, police officers, who had despicable wives. The women cheated on them, stole from them, lied to them, and then some. One trooper I know, announced in the squad room, that if he ever turned up dead, it was his wife. He was serious. I realize women don't have the corner on this market of duplicity. I know more than a few guys who did the very same thing.

Don't turn your back to the door at the restaurant, or on the guy wearing the same uniform. Keep your ducks in a row, and keep the emails you think you should keep; especially when dealing with problematic supervisors. When intuition tells you something is not right, listen.

Double check, be suspicious, do your work like you were trained to, don't cut corners, and most of all go home at the end of your shift. You might also want to stop in at home unexpectedly. Oh yeah, keep a real close eye on your finances. Those who have been burned financially often keep separate bank accounts. It would be wise to do that anyway.

The bottom line is this: humanity, as a rule, is not trust-worthy. The most famous man in history did not entrust himself to people, because he knew what was in them. His words are known all over this planet; they are probably worth considering.

SUPERVISORS

There are bosses that you'd run into a burning building for, and there are those who'd be found holding the lighter. In the middle of those two types are the easy-going bosses. Supervisors fall into one of these three categories, men and women alike. Once you've seen a supervisor with a lighter in hand, steer clear. If you don't think that people who have spent their careers pretending and trying to look good in a uniform, aren't gonna do whatever it takes to uphold their image; think again.

In my experience the good supervisors, who default to having your back, are outnumbered three to one. I've witnessed supervisors lying, because they got caught looking like the tools they are. Evidently, the little guy on my shoulder observed this as well. He saved my ass more than a few times; from supervisors and semi-trucks.

SUPERVISORS: PART DEUCE

So, a new supervisor had been transferred into the same post where I was ass-signed. It's generally not a good thing to get called into the boss's office. However, in celebration of their transfer, I got a personal invitation to sit in one of the two chairs in the office de-la-boss.

"Hello trooper, I'd like to welcome myself to this work location by chewing your ass like bubblegum."

"No trooper, I've never won the MADD[10] nomination for most drunk driver arrests at the post in a year."

"No, I've not knocked off big loads of cocaine or marijuana on the freeway."

"No, I haven't obtained confessions from suspects, and don't know how."

"No, I haven't chased suspects on foot through the not-so-nice parts of town after dark; in fact, I don't think I have chased anyone, for any reason, ever."

"No trooper, I make it a practice not to wrestle with suspects in the middle of the street or anywhere for that matter. I have, however, delivered a lot of paperwork to the court and done my fair share of school programs."

"Therefore, I'll chew on your ass for a while, to impress the real boss. Have a nice day trooper, I look forward to working with you."

Disclaimer:
The above statements may include inferences.

Sitting in the big boss's office, who was likely amused by this process, caused me to ponder his silence. He was on the way out, riding the slide down to retirement. At that point he was probably counting the days. Making waves was no longer a priority. That said, I have worked for bosses who would have tossed the bubblegum aficionado out of their office, and offered me a cup of coffee.

It was one of those moments that grows on you. It's a bit like the five steps of grief, only different. This process is called the three levels of response to BS from supervisors. The first response is anger. The second is ambivalence. The third and final stage is humor.

---

[10] Mothers Against Drunk Driving/external document

During the first stage; the non-sensical nature of the incident is abrasive and unpleasant for a period generally ranging between one to ten days. Phase two is rather like a number two. This phase smells unpleasant and lingers for a while like brown matter on porcelain. The final level is humor, increasing until it settles in as a smile inducing memory.

SUPERVISORS: PART DEUCE & ¼

On one particular occasion, a superior officer was getting squeezed by a prosecutor for mucking up a case. He tried to point the finger of responsibility for the foul-up in my direction for not giving him the proper information so that he could order an autopsy. Little did he know; I had kept the email that I had sent him, which advised of the details of the incident that had occurred several months earlier. I *knew* it would prove useful later. Apparently, he didn't think I knew who he really was. Leopards don't change their spots. I was contacted by the big boss's over the matter as the other supervisor had tried to put the onus on me. After I provided him with the email on his desk, the issue was put to rest. The boss-man looked at me with a curious look and asked me why I had kept that email from months prior. He shook his head, surprised, and left me to my work.

The little guy on my shoulder saved my ass again. I presume the prosecutor never got the update, and continued to think I was the culprit. I could have sent the email to the prosecutor, which proved who the guilty party was. The evidence was in my sent email box. I had the prosecutor's email address and all I had to do was click a button. But honestly, I didn't give a f#!% what the prosecutor thought. Years in a uniform produces thick skin.

SUPERVISORS:
PART DEUCE & ½

On another occasion, I did not listen to my intuition. This time it involved a supervisor who was so bright, he left his gun at home before going to serve a search warrant on a big felony case. Sir Forgets-a-lot forgot a lot of important shit, including a few things that dragged me into a discipline situation. Had I listened to my instincts and kept the information he might have ended up working in a cubicle with a wooden gun glued into his holster.

The disciplinary action was appealed at a department hearing that he had initiated. It did not go as he expected. Apparently, he didn't realize that some troopers investigate for a living. During the hearing I made a phone call over speaker phone, on the conference table, in the presence of the hearing officers. The call was to a federal agent. I asked him several questions and he corroborated my side of the story. All of it.

Anyway, the supervisor wound up with a clown face, and I got a piece of paper in my work file. I protested the paperwork but apparently clearing your name sometimes is subordinate to keeping a supervisor's reputation intact.

There's a saying that, "Those who can't do, teach." In police work it's often "Those who can't do, get promoted." Some of the striped sleeves or barred collars who have never been there nor done that, enjoy trying to grind the noses of those who have. Uniform warmers, who have not accomplished one tenth of the average officer, get off on being paper cuts in the fingers of those who work their asses off.

THERE HAS TO BE A BETTER WAY

Some people wonder why officers regularly look over their shoulders. Police officers, at least the good ones, arrest a horde of suspects during their careers (those who work in very rural areas don't have the same volume of criminals; but that doesn't mean there is no crime). In fact, some of the worst crimes I've heard of have happened within the jurisdiction of small police agencies.

Many of these arrestees are sent to prison for years, get deported, are felons that were involved in organized crime, or even members of notoriously violent Mexican drug cartels.

Speaking of cartels, their tentacles are spread all over this country. If you hear stories on the news of huge drug busts or enormous amounts of cash being seized; there is organized crime behind it, very likely Mexican cartels. You can call BS if you want, but I've seen it, as have guys I've worked with.

I knew an officer, who put a felon away for a long time. He was later informed that, while in prison, the suspect had tried to hire somebody to kill him. I know it was investigated, but I'm not sure of the outcome.

Police officers are informed whenever an officer is killed (at least the MSP had published this information daily, so I presume that other agencies did as well). The basic details of the incident were provided. The public has access to such information via the Officer Down Memorial Page: ODMP.org.

The names of police officers are conspicuously placed in arrest reports. I've often thought that this should be changed to numbers which would only be available via subpoena, and only to necessary personnel. In light of all of the information available on the internet, it wouldn't be difficult for criminals and organized crime to find these officers, their homes, and their families.

Sadly, it may take several tragedies before this is ever changed. There has to be a better way.

Chapter Twelve

DRUNKS

BLASTED

D ispatch had reported a really drunk driver on the freeway. We got lots of calls of suspected drunk drivers, but this guy was so drunk that he had somehow earned an urgent response. He had driven the wrong way on the freeway for a while, but eventually made it back to the correct side.

There's drunk, plastered, hammered, and then there's this guy. I found him on the highway, miraculously he had not killed anyone. He was stopped and arrested for drunk driving. At the time, a BAC (blood alcohol content) of .08 or over was sufficient to be arrested for drunk driving. I think my BAC increased just from talking to him. His level? Over .40.

The average Joe would be dead long before .40. Even professional drunks are slammed at a BAC of .30. This middle-aged fella was so drunk that the jail wouldn't take him. They didn't want the liability risk of tossing him in a cell and having him die from alcohol poisoning.

What do you do when the jail won't take the guy you arrested because he's too drunk? You take him to the hospital and wait until his BAC drops to a level that is acceptable to the jail. I spent an enjoyable few hours drunk sitting. In concept, it wasn't that much different from babysitting. The whole goal was to keep them from hurting themselves or others. I should've got extra brownie points in my performance appraisal for being a reliable "drunk sitter."

From the time a traffic stop is initiated, officers regularly spend about an hour processing a drunk driver. That time is spent evaluating sobriety tests, completing breath test or blood test paperwork, transport, the actual breath test or blood test, booking, fingerprints, photographs, and so on.

Occasionally a suspect would not submit to a breath or blood test. In that case a search warrant would be drafted, sent to a judge who reviewed and signed it. Then came the inevitable confrontation with the needle. The arrested subject had two options: 1) submit to the judge's order, and go along with the process 2) continue to buck the system. If they chose the second option, they would get to experience what it felt like to be held down by several adults while a phlebotomist used the large needle.

Those who chose to force an officer's hand into obtaining a search warrant, got a chance to see if the officer was bluffing. Since the overwhelming majority of drunk drivers were arrested during the night shift, the uncooperative drunk would get to look two state troopers in the eyes and consider a description of the process. They were brought to the intersection of the easy road, which maintains some semblance of dignity. Or the hard road, which includes me kneeling on your face while the nice lady over there does her job. The drunks may or may not have heard those very words. Very few people chose the hard road. I don't recall ever having to kneel on anyone's face, although the phrase was rather influential. We did, however have to physically restrain several adult children, while they were throwing tantrums.

Back to the extremely inebriated gent. He hadn't been driving around at 2:00 am (when the bars closed in Michigan). He was driving during the day. It was still daylight when I transported him from the hospital to the county jail. Some of the most highly intoxicated people I arrested were during the day shift.

F-BOMBS

Shock and awe. That's why F-bombs are dropped. Like flash-bangs they are used to stun and immediately command attention.

I had come from a fairly religious background and expletives weren't a part of my vocabulary. Then I worked the night shift. At this point I was still relatively green. My two partners and I were working a three-man rotation; in my opinion it was a ridiculous schedule, and a poor use of resources.

Anyway, back to the point. While I was watching my language, as I had been taught, I was also watching each of my partners using the verbal tool tactically and effectively. It wasn't long before I had appropriated this tool. It hung on my gun belt, next to my cuffs, and pepper spray.

There is a notable difference between "Put your hands up," and "Put your fucking hands up." I became rather adept at using my new-found ability. Sailors would have been impressed. Hey, if you find something that works, why not become proficient at it.

I went back and forth in my career over the frequency with which this tactic would be deployed. I finally settled in at trying not to use it unless it was necessary given the situation. But never did it get removed from my tool belt, unlike my collapsible baton.

Later in my career, I worked in a different area, with a different partner, but still on the night shift. I was generally laid-back, so some of the people I worked with were occasionally shocked to see me dropping a rare F-bomb. This particular partner was not a burning ball of motivation; he made my laid-back look like that of an amateur.

It was my night to drive, and we stopped a car for suspected drunk driving. The smell of alcohol permeated the air around the car, like it usually did when dealing with drunks. We dealt with drunks so regularly that we could often tell if the driver was headed to jail simply by the potency of the strength of the smell of intoxicants in the air, even before speaking with the driver.

I began talking with the driver through his window. Meanwhile, up speaks the inebriated ass-clown in the back seat. He was seated next to his drunk girlfriend who mouthed off too as she was half climbed onto the clown's lap. I attempted to continue my conversation with the driver, beginning to evaluate his level of intoxication.

The drunk twenty-something in the rear seat, decided he was going to direct the verbal traffic, and started spouting the typical nonsense; why did you stop us, he's not drunk, don't you got anything better to do, and so on.

I stopped him mid-motormouth with the effective phrase, "Hey asshole, shut the fuck up." The three occupants of the car sat in silence. The linguistic Kung-Fu had its intended impact. The bottom line is sometimes serious language gets the point across when it wouldn't happen otherwise.

My partner, who was standing on the passenger side of the vehicle, may have been as shocked as the inebriated trio. You'd think I just did the Matrix kick or something. He looked at me in disbelief. I'm not sure if it was because he didn't think that would come out of me, or if he didn't have that tool packed on his gun belt. Either way, he became aware that I could and would use it when necessary.

The driver was arrested, and José Cuervo, from the back seat, apparently decided that a closed mouth was a better alternative than jail.

TWOFERS

On yet another night shift, my partner and I were patrolling at prime drunk time, when the bars closed. We followed a vehicle until it turned into the Taco Bell drive thru. The two occupants got their chalupas. They also decided they'd switch drivers.

Again, we followed the girls with the midnight munchies. The car was stopped for some traffic violation. The ladies admitted that one of them had driven into the fast food parking lot, and the other had driven out.

One drunk arrest for each trooper. Night shift officers know the drunk driver arrest program well, because we've all done it so often. It's fair to say that during the night shift, the offense we most often arrested people for was drunk driving.

This same scenario happened one other time in my career, while assigned to a different post. We were following a vehicle driven by large male with a petite female as a passenger. The driver and passenger actually switched seats while still driving. This was clearly visible due to the street lights in the area plus our headlights. We stopped the inebriated couple as they pulled into a gas station.

Two troopers, one traffic stop, and two drunks arrested, twice.

BIRDIES, EAGLES, & BIG WHEELS

On a few rare occasions, we would have one subject in custody for drunk driving, and be headed to the jail when we had to stop another. It's policy to take an arrested subject to the jail as soon as possible. You're responsible for them until they are at the jail, and are unavailable for other incidents. However, letting another obvious drunk driver continue to drive, is a legitimate danger to the public. Two drunk drivers in custody during the same trip to the jail, would generally impress the jail guards.

In the game of golf, birdies are fairly rare at least by amateurs. At one of my worksites we regarded 'birdies' as two drunk driving arrests in the same shift. The ever elusive 'eagle', was three drunk drivers arrested during one shift. A few night shift partners and I snagged three in one night, but not very often. Three drunks arrested in an eight-hour shift is likely less common than an 'eagle' is in golf.

Night shift occasionally provided for some unusual events. One of which happened in the parking lot of a local restaurant, which catered to the drunk crowd after the bars closed. This business was near the main road through the city.

My partner and I happened to be within eyeshot of that parking lot. We watched a Jeep with oversized tires, doing tricks in the parking lot. The best one included driving one tire up onto the cement base of a steel light post, then parked there. The top of the concrete support for the light was at least a foot tall, if not closer to two feet. It was a cool trick, I admit. It was, however, probably not the wisest choice to drive up light posts while a few troopers are watching. It was like the vehicular version of a pole dance.

The Jeep trickster received a ticket for driving while dumb. He should have stuck with BMX bikes and skateboards.

Unchecked, extreme stress is an emotional and physical carnivore. It chews hungrily on so many of our law enforcement officers with its razor-sharp fangs, and does so quietly, silently in every corner of their lives. It affects their job performance, their relationships and ultimately their health. In World War I, World War II, and Korea, the number of soldiers who pulled out of the front lines because they were psychiatric casualties was greater than the number of those who died in combat.

- Lt. Col. David Grossman, *On Combat*

Chapter Thirteen

TRAUMA

THE TRIBULATIONS OF TRAUMA

The premise of Dr. Van Der Kolk's book, *The Body Keeps Score*, is that the experience of trauma(s) can have profound effects upon the human body and mind. MRI's can often reveal damage in the brains of those who have been traumatized. The subconscious is impacted, as well as the conscious mind. After three decades of studying trauma, and its various impacts on patients, the doctor has become one of the premier experts in this field.

> *"...in the Country Library at Harvard Medical School, I discovered The Traumatic Neuroses of War, which had been published in 1941 by a psychiatrist named Abram Kardiner. It described Kardiner's observations of (WWI) veterans and had been released in anticipation of the flood of shell-shocked soldiers expected to be casualties of (WWII).*
>
> *Kardiner reported the same phenomena I was seeing: After the war his patients were overtaken by a sense of futility; they became withdrawn and detached, even if they had functioned well before. What Kardiner called "traumatic neuroses," today we call post-traumatic stress disorder-PTSD. Kardiner noted that sufferers from traumatic neuroses develop a chronic vigilance for and sensitivity to threat. His summation especially caught my eye: "<u>The nucleus of the neurosis is a physioneuroisis</u>." <u>In other words, post-traumatic stress isn't "all in one's head," as</u>*

179

*some people supposed, but has a physiological basis. Kardiner
understood even then that the symptoms have their origin in the
entire body's response to the original trauma.*"[11]

Police officers and frontline soldiers alike, regularly encounter death, serious injuries, and a variety of extremely
dangerous situations. These defenders of society are not the
only people in our world who experience these types of situations and/or great tragedies. Our newspaper headlines are
filled with the stories of violent and devastating events. People who were abused or experienced even a single traumatic
incident can suffer lifelong problems as a result. Not everyone experiences the same symptoms, nor the same levels of
severity. Some of the persistent problems which include, but
are not limited to are:

Sleep problems, nightmares, flashbacks, anxiety, trust issues, hyper-vigilance, worst case scenario thinking, irritabil-
ity, memory issues, depression, suicidal thoughts, isolation,
and a host of others. Physical symptoms include brain damage, increased blood pressure/heart rate, shallow breathing,
shaking, and more.

This condition can also occasionally result in autoimmune
diseases.[12]

INVISIBLE WOUNDS

As I sat in the passenger seat of my training officer's patrol
car, I showed him a boot knife which one of my friends had
purchased for me after graduating from the academy.

He said to me, "You know what that's for right?"

I responded, "Cutting seatbelts, and maybe self-defense."

"It is for jamming into the forehead of someone who is at
tacking you." He stated.

---

[11] Bessel Van Der Kolk, MD., *The Body Keeps Score,* p. 11
[12] Ibid. p. 53

At that point I was still trying to get accustomed to his words relating police work to war.

He told me to look around. I did. Then he stated that any one of the people who I saw, could have a reason, and a plan to kill a police officer. He said police officers are murdered all across our country. It doesn't happen every day, but it does happen. He explained that I always needed to be aware of my surroundings. This officer took the job at face value; as deadly serious as it is.

While I was stunned at the time, this was a worthwhile lesson. He was training me for a career in which I would always be armed, and could involve response to literally any circumstance. His words echoed the training I had received at the academy.

ODMP.org provides statistics regarding how many law enforcement officers have died during the line of duty, and how. In 2016 the total number was 161, in 2017 the number was 137, many of them were murdered.

Every shift I loaded a long gun into my car, be it a rifle or a shotgun, sometimes both. Some people despise police officers simply for wearing the uniform. Like so many lessons that he taught me, experience would add tremendous weight to his words. I would encounter people with guns, violent criminals, gang-bangers, drug couriers, felons, a plethora of parolee's, and more.

The MSP provided us with weapons for a reason. Also, a specially tailored bulletproof vest. The trunk of the patrol car included a large first aid kit, an AED (automated external defibrillator), fire extinguisher, ax, crowbar etc. Each of these had a purpose, and each were used.

It was the very next day after the fatal crash, (Which I placed in the next chapter under the heading: *A Day I Wish I Could Forget*) and I was at the post getting ready for my shift. A thirty-year veteran detective and mentor spoke with me. He said I'd be alright, and that I'd respond to the same situation if it happened again that day. His words went straight through me. I was still trying to process the traumatic death of a little girl, the devastation it had brought into the lives of her parents, the gruesome nature of the scene, and the trauma of it all. It was like he had kicked me while I was already down. He wasn't intentionally trying to cause harm, but he was a seasoned warrior who knew this from experience. It was the truth of those words, which was so painful. He was right. That call could come again at any moment, and I would respond.

I lived trauma. We all did. The police radio could potentially call out any number of emergency situations, and at any time. The emergency tones from dispatch became an anxiety-producing sound. It had the effect of a tornado siren, announcing a massive storm.

It's probably fair to say that, to a certain extent, we all felt that way. Who wants to be thrust into the path of a tornado? New guys tend to get excited when those calls came out. Yet many veterans hated that sound. We would go. We would respond. We would often even go into the jurisdiction of other agencies to help; municipalities and townships, etc., they also would come to help us.

In a manner similar to how the various tragedies impacted families, so also the compilation of years of traumatic events effect police officers. I am no exception.

Most frontline soldiers can only stand the heat of battle for so long. Many come back with scars that are not physical. One of my friends who had been in the military and who was a kick-ass cop, told me, "Not all wounds are visible." He was right.

Like an officer shot in the hip, or the hand, or the torso, who've been run over by cars (guys I know). Like those who suffered physical wounds that would impact them for the rest of their lives; so also, with these types of injuries that are not visible.

Those who have these ghostly wounds will find that the overwhelming majority of people who have not fought these battles cannot understand. Humanity, as a rule finds it almost impossible to genuinely comprehend what someone suffers with, if they themselves have not experienced it.

I cannot truly grasp the depths of what my cousin suffered when she was diagnosed with, and treated for severe cancer. It would be impossible for me to understand the thoughts and emotional pain of my uncle who slowly died from ALS. All I can do is imagine. These were medical conditions that were visible, and had physical effects. No amount of words can produce an adequate understanding of such suffering. If we cannot genuinely apprehend, and fully appreciate the magnitude of the pain and anguish of those with conditions which are visible, how much less with men and women who suffer with invisible afflictions?

Like a contagion, trauma often begets trauma.

VIGILANCE

These soldiers of our society live on the edge of life and death, and as a result generally become very aware of their own mortality maybe even too much so. It is reasonable to conclude that this is one of the conditions which enables heroes to jump on grenades to save their buddies, or to run into skyscrapers which have been hit by commercial jets.

Knowing that each day could be your last, combined with legitimate concern for those standing next to you (and the pubic), impacts your decision making. This is no doubt part of the reason why police officers and soldiers alike often do things that are heroic. Their concern for themselves has been moved to the back of the bus, in order that the safety of others may be moved to the front. This mindset is birthed on the battlefield, not in ivory towers.

Hyper-vigilance is often a result of much time spent on the front lines. On a multitude of occasions, this proved to be

183

personally problematic; like when I was with my wife at the store, or out for lunch together. She quickly tired of this effect on me. Pleasant dinners at nice restaurants became less than pleasant, as she watched me eyeballing people inside, as well as cars in the parking lot. I increasingly disliked going out, she also started to like it less when I went with her.

After a career serving on the front lines of law enforcement, I had developed a symbiotic relationship with this survival sense. Little did I know I would not be able to turn it off.

UNTRUSTED

Friends, family, and coworkers whom I had previously trusted, began to be viewed through the lens with which I observed the rest of the world: untrustworthy. My skeptical eyes watched them as I constantly evaluated motivations. Family members occasionally caught a mouthful, as I am excessively overprotective of my children, and don't want them in certain situations. None of this had been a problem prior to my career, or even early in my career.

Previously I cared too much about what my family and friends thought. Offensiveness in this regard has become significantly less concerning. The little guy on my shoulder doesn't trust anyone, and is perpetually on the lookout for trouble.

It used to be that I was too trusting. I don't have that problem anymore.

Chapter Fourteen

VEHICLE CRASHES

Police officers respond to two types of vehicular accidents: in Michigan they were referred to as a PDA (property damage accident) or PIA (personal injury accident). This chapter includes only the latter, specifically those I responded to which resulted in fatalities. There were other fatal crashes which have not been included. However, those which follow were among the most traumatic encountered during my career. The following stories contain graphic content.

MOTORCYCLE VS. CAR

I was working a night shift with one of the senior troopers at the post when we responded to the scene of a car vs. motorcycle crash. We were at the scene a while before the life flight helicopter arrived. It was from a metropolitan hospital with a highly rated trauma center.

The young man who had been driving the motorcycle crashed into a vehicle that had pulled out in front of him. He was laying in the road when we arrived. Members of the fire department marked out a landing zone for the helicopter with flares. Out came the combat medics. This crew knew what the hell they were doing, as do all such crews, at least in my experience.

185

As they worked on the victim, I asked what I could do to help. I was requested to hold a flashlight over the young man's chest. As I did, I observed one of the medics insert a large needle into the side of man's chest. I asked if she could answer questions or if I should just shut up and let her do her job. She responded that she had no problem explaining the what she was doing.

She spoke while she worked like a professional. I don't know how many times she had done this, but I presume it was a multitude, given that she was able to have a conversation with me while being totally focused on the man lying on the concrete. There were others treating the man as well. It wasn't long before the man was loaded up into the helicopter, and off they flew. The young man would not survive his injuries.

I was still relatively new at the time, and was struck by the experience. It was a scene straight out of a military movie, one which would become all too familiar.

ONE OF THE DAYS
I WISH I COULD FORGET

It was a sunny day with very few clouds, and I had loaded my patrol car and got out of the post quick that day. It was around shift change and the squad room was full. My shift started at 2:00pm or 3:00pm that day.

I headed out onto the freeway, which had three lanes each way. Traffic was so thick that running radar would be pointless. Traffic enforcement was fairly enjoyable during pleasant weather. But that day the freeway tickets were gonna have to wait until later. I exited the freeway. Then the emergency tones rang out over the radio.

The dispatcher advised that a semi-truck had crossed the median and collided with oncoming traffic. I was only a few miles away, and screamed back onto the freeway, pushing the patrol car to the level it was designed for. I was there within a minute or two, and first on scene.

It was carnage.

The westbound semi-truck had blasted through the narrow median and crossed all three of the eastbound lanes, ending up well off of the freeway. Traffic was already stopped. Two eastbound cars had been involved in the crash.

As soon as I exited my patrol car, I saw her on the grassy area near shoulder of the highway, well away from the location of the collision. It took only a split second to see that the child was dead. I turned my head away because of the gruesome trauma. Someone on scene had the presence of mind to quickly cover her body with an emergency blanket. It was probably a truck driver. They often carried some emergency equipment with them. I was grateful that the parents would not have to see her in that condition.

I called out on the portable radio hanging from my hip, "Send everyone." It may have been the only time I ever uttered that phrase over the radio. Other officers and emergency personnel arrived on scene. Traffic had come to a standstill.

I'll never forget hearing the voices screaming out, "Where is my daughter?" "Where is my little girl?"

I saw an adult male and female walking around the freeway searching, scanning, and yelling for her. The dispatchers later reported being able to hear those screams during some of my radio traffic. I saw their van and knew. Some crash scenes quickly reveal what happened, this was one of those. Their van had been sliced in half, from the driver's door, diagonally back through to the center of the rear hatch.

Despite already knowing, I asked them if that was their van, and they confirmed that it was. They were frantic. I looked at one of my respected friends, who wore the same uniform as me. We communicated without words. We knew someone had to tell them.

I knelt in the middle of the highway, and reached for the mother's hand. She held my hand, with her other hand over her mouth. Tears flowed down her face. I could see the father a few feet back, in obvious shock. I told them. "She's gone. Your little girl is dead." She fell to her knees weeping. How do you comfort someone in such a moment? She wrapped her arms around me, and wept.

Another vehicle was involved in the wreckage, and it had not been hit by the semi, but had unique damage. There was a hole in the windshield about the size of a football, and another similar sized hole the back window as well. Human remains were spread across the front of the vehicle, including the interior. The occupants of that vehicle were unharmed, but traumatized. Later while speaking to another officer who helped investigate the details of the accident scene, I was advised that the second vehicle had been declared totaled by the insurance company simply because of the amount of biohazard.

I contacted the semi driver. He was still seated in his truck, which was well beyond the freeway, and into the ditch. He was either in stunned shock himself, or did not care what he had just done. I was livid, and headed to the hospital with the truck driver for a blood sample. Just before I drove away, a senior trooper looked at me and offered to take the report himself. He was serious, and I knew it. But I couldn't put this burden on someone else's shoulders. I thanked him and told him I'd take it.

While at the hospital, after I had completed what needed to be done. I saw the family of the deceased, in one of the hospital rooms. I needed to give them a business card and report number. Several people were in the room, as I walked in. The agony was tangible. I briefly conveyed my condolences and fought back tears with all my strength. I choked out a few words and gave someone the business card. What else could I do? Nothing, and I knew it. If I had stayed to offer some level of support, I would have begun crying myself, and only added to their pain.

Days later, it occurred to me that because of how thick the traffic was that day, it could have been a dozen cars which were hit. If it's possible to find any solace in that catastrophic event; it was the fact that there were not a multitude of fatalities. There very well could have been.

Grace in the midst of devastation.

OFFICERS DO CRY

On another bright and sunny day. The emergency tones went off, and the call was for a child that had been run over by a car. I wasn't far away. A local officer was first on scene, I arrived shortly after him. A young child (maybe three years old) had been backed over by a car in the driveway. The driver was an unsuspecting family member.

The medics quickly had the child loaded into the ambulance and were attempting to stabilize her. The other officer and I spoke briefly, and agreed this incident was urgent enough for us to escort the ambulance to the hospital. An ambulance escort involved officers speeding ahead of the ambulance and blocking an intersection in order that the medics wouldn't have to slow down. The whole idea was to help the medics get to the hospital faster.

I was starting to get angry, because the ambulance wasn't leaving. I yelled at the medics and offered to drive their rig to the hospital while they attended to the child. They declined my offer and advised they were trying to stabilize the child sufficiently for them to begin transport.

Moments later the ambulance took off. The local officer and I took turns passing the ambulance and blocking traffic at the next intersection. One intersection blocked, the other officer would fly past and block the next. We did this for at least twenty miles and through maybe a dozen intersections.

The medics arrived at the hospital much faster than they would have otherwise. The emergency room personnel were ready to receive the child. The officer and I entered the hospital. Shortly thereafter we departed side by side. I saw tears rolling down his face. I was numb. My heart hurt, I should have cried, but I couldn't. We both had young ones at home. Images from that scene have been burned into my memory.

The child made it to the hospital alive, but died shortly thereafter. Ever since that incident, I've been obsessive about knowing where my children are before anybody drives out of our driveway.

CAR VS. TREE

The rain was coming down steadily on a night shift that would prove to be unforgettable. One of the local police departments had responded to a dispatched priority call of a car vs. tree collision. My partner and I headed in that direction to assist.

Upon arrival I saw the car that had smashed head on into a massive tree. The vehicle had lost control, in the rain, on a curve. The driver was already deceased but there was someone else trapped in the wreckage.

Emergency first responders flooded the scene to assist. The fire departments, whether volunteer or full time, were always immensely helpful. There were several firemen on scene. Fire departments have equipment that is designed to tear cars apart, they also have hydraulic presses in order to un-crush damaged vehicles enough to remove any trapped occupants. They were invaluable, whether they came and assisted with traffic control, or to use their emergency equipment, quench various fires, and clear the roadway of debris, or chemicals. I can't say enough about how priceless these men and women are to our society, and so many of them are volunteers.

None of their equipment was successful in trying to remove the injured passenger, whose leg was pinned into the car. He appeared to be in and out of consciousness. The experienced, senior medic on scene called the Emergency Room doctor. He received instructions to amputate the subject's leg in an effort to save his life.

This was an order that stunned all of us. All of us present at the scene probably had combined total of over one hundred years of emergency response experience, if not two hundred. Yet, nobody on scene had experienced this before. Seasoned men turned their heads away from the traumatic sight.

The passenger was unable to speak, but he was moving around a little; his right hand was free to move. The passenger side door had either been removed or torn open, either way we could see the interior of the car through the passenger door area.

I saw the medic with a scalpel in his hand and an intense look upon his face. He was about to do something incredibly rare and courageous in order to attempt to save this guy's life. I knew that the medic couldn't do his job with the passenger's arm flailing around. So, I laid on the ground and held the man's hand; both to secure it and to offer some level of human contact. I don't know if he could tell I was there, probably not. Honestly, I tried not to look too, but it was unavoidable given the urgent nature of the circumstances.

We were trained and experienced in triaging situations. Police officers, firemen, and medics arrive on scene, see a need and get to work. I'm certain that if I didn't hold onto that man's hand, somebody would have. I saw a job that needed to be done, so that the medic could do the much more difficult task.

The medic did his job well. The passenger's leg was amputated at a place where there was a severe break. The victim was finally able to be removed from the vehicle. The medics rushed him off to the hospital. However, the subject eventually succumbed to his injuries.

Some images never leave your mind. This incident, like so many others has a series of images, which have become flashbacks. Sometimes they resurface; without warning.

THE LAST CONVERSATION

It was a nasty snow storm and road conditions were terrible. Traffic was generally light on the highway during the nightshift and even more so during blizzards. I don't recall if it was a priority dispatched call of an accident or just a report of a vehicle in the ditch. Either way, we were not that far away from the scene. We drove as fast as weather and road conditions would permit. I may have been able to run faster.

Once we arrived on scene, I saw the small single cab pickup partially wrapped around a tree, sideways. There were four occupants in the truck. One of the four, on the side of the truck that hit the tree was visibly dead; his head had hit the tree. We had called out the severity of the crash to dispatch. I advised we would need the fire department, and their equipment.

We waited for what seemed like forever for the fire department. We spoke to the three occupants, trying to keep them as calm and distracted as possible in the terrible circumstances. My partner and I used our crowbar to try to pry the door open, but it wouldn't budge.

Due to the nasty road conditions it took the fire department an unusually long time to arrive on scene. We were still talking with the occupants and trying to pry the door open when they arrived. As the firemen used their specialized equipment, to pry open the door, one of the female occupants died. We had been speaking with her, and the other two, when she faded into unconsciousness and died from her injuries.

The fire department cut the vehicle apart, and the other two occupants were removed. They were transported to the hospital and each survived.

An autopsy was ordered. I was directed to attend, and went with a few other troopers. It remains an entirely unforgettable ordeal, from the crash scene through to the autopsy. I cannot describe the impact of seeing the lady who I had recently been speaking with, lying deceased on a large metal table in the morgue. The other deceased passenger was there as well, also on a table.

That was one of the days which my training officer had described. I certainly wouldn't volunteer go through it again, even if offered ten thousand dollars to do so.

"Taking your own life… Interesting expression. Taking it from who? Once it's over it's not you who will miss it. Your own death is something that happens to everyone else. Your life is not your own, keep your hands off it."

- Sherlock Holmes
SHERLOCK, Season 4, 2017

Chapter Fifteen

SUICIDE

THE TRAGIC NATURE OF SUICIDE

I have been on too many suicide scenes, although one is too many. The first one was with a senior officer. An older man had parked in any empty lot, exited his truck, and shot himself in the chest with a rifle. While the scene wasn't particularly gruesome, it was disturbing. They all were.

Intense pain and personal troubles are clearly the primary motivations behind people ending their own lives. Anyone who has been in any way acquainted with a suicide, has witnessed the trail of devastation it leaves behind.

One case was discovered on a night shift by my partner and I. He drove into a parking lot to check on the only car in the lot. Seated in the driver's seat was a middle-aged man who was obviously deceased. He had used some sort of grill device in the back of the car, and gassed himself to death. Upon contact with family members, we were advised that the deceased gentleman had a son who had killed himself years ago, on that same date.

A TEENAGE BOY

A municipal police officer was dispatched to the scene of a suicide. I had known the officer for years, and was in the area. It would have been selfish, and irresponsible to leave him to handle such a situation alone, so I responded and went to assist him. A teenager had shot himself with his father's gun. The family was not home at the time, and had come back to find the gruesome scene.

There are no words to describe the level of desperation and devastation which racked the family members. The officer covered the bases with his investigation. Meanwhile I was somebody for the mother to hug on and weep. It took a while for the officer to take care of his responsibilities, and then for the body of the deceased to be removed by local funeral home personnel.

In an inconsolable situation, the family was comforted by our presence and empathy; in as much as this was possible considering the horrible circumstances. Other friends and/or family members arrived, and took over that role.

Leaving the distraught family, before others arrived to support them, seemed heartless. We couldn't do it. Silent support is meaningful in such a situation, even if it is from strangers.

A CANCER PATIENT

The dispatcher had sent a nearby officer to the scene of a suicide. I arrived to assist as did another officer or two. I can't imagine that an officer would prefer to deal with such situations alone, I know I wouldn't.

The deceased subject was a middle-aged male cancer patient. The painful road ahead of him was evidently more than he could bear, and he had shot himself in the chest with a rifle. Family members knew he was suffering, but hadn't expected this.

They were understandably grieved by the incident. Who wouldn't be? That room of the house would no doubt be a reminder of the troublesome image, and memory.

196

A TEENAGE GIRL

One of the most difficult of these situations, for me personally, was the case of a young teenage girl who had hung herself. She had done so in a seated position, from a door knob in her bedroom. Her mother found her and was beyond inconsolable. A deputy had arrived before me, and as such I was there to assist him. The girl was visibly dead. The obvious painful nature of the incident, was only multiplied by seeing the mother so distressed. I presume this case was unusually distressing for me to handle, because I had a child at home as well.

It is well known among law enforcement that traumatic incidents involving children are the most difficult to deal with. I presume that in this case, I was less than helpful to the deputy. I don't know if I wanted the mother to see us at least try to resuscitate her daughter; despite knowing that it would be a futile effort, and possibly even make it more painful for the mother. I don't know if I was in a state of shock myself because of the intensely traumatic nature of this particular incident. Whatever it was, I wasn't helpful to the deputy, like I normally would have been. This one still haunts me. Sometimes I still see her face, and the way she was seated in her room. Flashbacks are not uncommon for traumatic incidents. This was one such case. I have to force myself to think of something else. Even writing about it is painful. Yet I hope getting it out on paper will help lay the incident to rest in my subconscious. Experience tells me that it won't.

EVEN POLICE OFFICERS

A trooper that I had known killed himself. I don't know all the details, and don't want to. But I had heard that nobody saw it coming.

Another trooper, whose name I had heard before but never knew, also committed suicide. I also heard the story of another who ended his life shortly after he retired.

I know two officers who, on different occasions, each watched a man shoot himself. Most, if not all, of the officers I worked with had stories of suicide cases which they had dealt with. Several of those accounts were of gruesome scenes. I won't describe them. There is no pleasure in talking about such things. Yet, apparently officers needed to get the emotions out in words, even if they didn't know it.

Police officers are trained to be the strong ones. They are trained to respond to any type of dispatched call for service. Officers are the people that others look to for help, and as such, they are often not willing to seek help for themselves. Alcohol regularly becomes a means of self-medication. More than a few have succumbed to the battle with the bottle.

THERE WERE OTHERS

These weren't the only suicides that I encountered during my career. Reporting the others would be superfluous. The point is that suicide is a horrible thing. It is terrible to witness as an officer, or otherwise. More significantly, it is catastrophic and traumatic for family and friends. Some of them will never fully recover from the wounds which these events have spawned.

There is no way I can understand the details of all of these situations. I only witnessed the aftermath. Very often, these incidents left me with the sense that it was a deeply selfish act.

Conversations with children and loved ones regarding this issue would be more than prudent. Many teenagers consider such actions; their hormones are raging, heartbreaks are a common occurrence at that age, and bullying is a regular problem. Adults also need to have conversations about this. While working, I have spoken with several people who

198

were admitted into hospitals for considering this as a legitimate solution to their troubles. It's not. It's selfish, and
leaves terrible devastation and pain in its wake.

*"Suicide doesn't end the chances of life getting worse, it
eliminates the possibility of it ever getting any better."*
- Unknown

"You can't handle the truth."

\- A few Good Men, 1992

Chapter Sixteen

COURT

PROSECUTORS & JUDGES

In Michigan, the chief prosecutor was the head law enforcement officer in the county. They were generally aided by a number of assistant prosecutors, who carried the overwhelming majority of the workload.

A good prosecutor is priceless. A bad one can sink your case, like a torpedo attack on a battleship. I have seen both. Thankfully the good ones outnumber the bad ones nine to one, at least in my experience. Like any job does, experience makes for better prosecuting attorneys.

The vast majority of criminal cases get pled out long before they would have gone to trial: basically, the suspect pleads guilty, often to a lesser charge, for an arrangement that reduces their punishment.

Watching a good prosecuting attorney in action is like watching an artist at work. They are first class, intense, able to think on their feet, anticipate the moves of the defense, and often blow them out of the water.

In my career, I had only a dozen or so cases which went to trial. Most of which involved drunk driving arrests. Often times the defendant had a high dollar attorney, with slicked back hair; you know the guy, whose face is plastered on billboards or on ridiculous commercials. I encountered a few of those guys who were at the defense table as I sat at the prosecutor's table. I had a front row seat to watch a prosecutor work their magic.

It is said that once a jury is sworn in, you can never tell what's gonna happen. Sometimes a jury's decision is like the flip of a coin. Half of the time it will come up like you called it. Well, it's almost like that. A solid case and a good prosecutor are like the two hands of a boxing champ. But sometimes even the champs get beat.

Several judges I had observed while doing their jobs were brilliant. It was one of the all-pro judges, from whom I first heard the phrase, "The nature of law is that it requires voluntary compliance." This is now an obvious truth to me, but when I first heard it, I was impressed with its precision. Those who don't voluntarily comply, eventually end up in front of guys like him.

GOLF BUDDIES

There's a reason attorneys golf with judges, or bowl, or play badminton. Whatever the judge's hobby, some defense attorneys occasionally try to work their way in, to rub elbows with the people in the black robes. Sometimes it pays off. On one occasion this was evident.

Another trooper and I had obtained reliable information that there was a guy in town who was slinging a significant amount of cocaine. The trooper and I contacted the homeowners/grandparents where the twenty-something male suspect lived.

The suspect wasn't home at the time. The grandmother of the suspect advised that he lived in an upstairs bedroom, and that she regularly went in there to bring in his laundry. Because the homeowner had unrestricted access to the suspects bedroom, he had no expectation of privacy there. There was caselaw to back this up. The grandparents both gave us permission to enter his bedroom and look around.

This was rather early in my career so I hadn't learned to keep a digital voice recorder in my shirt pocket. However, I did have another trooper present with me, who witnessed both homeowners give us verbal consent.

It didn't take long for us to locate a plastic baggie with a golf ball sized chunk of white powdery substance. He probably wasn't keeping baggies of flour for making cookies. At that point we stopped looking. The other trooper remained in the home and secured the room, while I obtained a search warrant to continue the search.

The search warrant was obtained, and I returned to the residence with the paperwork in hand. At this point the suspect's mother had shown up. She stood in my way and told me I wasn't searching anything. She demanded to see the search warrant. I splained her that because she didn't live in the home, she didn't have to see anything. She was pissed. Mom got quick instructions to sit down and be quiet or she would have some assistance leaving the property or maybe even get a free ride to the county jail. Mother of the year didn't understand that there were laws about interfering with a police investigation.

A dealer-level quantity of drugs, and at least one gun was found in the suspect's bedroom. I presume the grandparents were surprised about this. Felony charges were sought and the suspect later located and arrested.

The other trooper and I each had been subpoenaed to one of the pre-trial hearings on this case. A new prosecutor and a defense attorney who was a golf-buddy of the judge, combined for a dismissal of the case. The judge didn't think the word of two state troopers was more believable than that of the grandma and grandpa who wanted to keep their boy out of trouble.

Thankfully, I only witnessed this once.

*It is not good to be partial to the wicked
or to deprive the righteous of justice.*
- Proverbs 18:5

THE NICE DEFENSE ATTORNEY

Of all of my cases that ever went to trial, there's one checkmark in the loss column. It was a drunk driving case. A reasonable person would conclude that the suspect was blitzed and driving.

My night shift partner and I responded to a dispatched call of a drunk subject driving around a residence repeatedly and screaming at someone inside the house. The vehicle description was provided.

We arrived on scene to find a highly intoxicated female standing outside of a running vehicle which matched a description of her car. I contacted her and she told me she had locked her keys in her car and asked me to unlock it for her. She failed to realize that her driver side window was open. There was sufficient probable cause to believe that she was the one driving the vehicle registered in her name including her own admission and the statement of the person inside the house who had called 911.

Weak spots in the case were exploited: A) my partner was unavailable to testify B) I had no video due to an inconsistent VCR in the trunk. In this case a sharp defense attorney, not the guy on the billboard, used his nice guy skills to raise enough reasonable doubt for the jury to come back with a not guilty verdict.

In my experience, defense attorneys generally didn't use the nice guy routine. In this case the guy wasn't acting, he genuinely was a nice guy. He did his job well. Years later, I bumped into him and said hello. He asked how I knew his name. I told him that it was because he was the only guy I had ever lost to in a trial.

Chapter Seventeen

NOTES FROM THE WIFE

Being the wife of a state trooper is not all sexy uniforms and happy time. Although, I must admit that he did look devilishly handsome all suited up.

The day that I met my husband, the moment our eyes met was fireworks. Cliché, I know, but it really was. Somehow, I knew this badass-looking mother scratcher was the man I was meant to spend the rest of my life with. The rest, well, let's just say that is an interesting story, but would give away too many details of who we are. Anonymity is what we both really want.

One of the events I remember the most is when he came home looking all sorts of grungy, not having showered in a few days and, if I had not known any better all strung out (he wasn't, FYI). He had a big grin splattered all over his face, and I asked him how his day was.

"I bought my first meth today!"

My response was something you wouldn't normally reply to a loved one who just admitted to buying meth. I told him, "I'm so proud of you! Good job!" or something to that effect, then gave him a big hug.

I was really, genuinely proud of him. I believe that if you sell something like meth you should end up in something similar to *Escape from New York*. Great movie by the way, I love Kurt Russell.

I knew the gist of what he did while working undercover, but in order to protect our family I never really asked for details. Plus, ignorance is bliss as they say, and in this case it was for me.

Several of the traumatic events that my husband experienced were before I ever had the honor of meeting him, so I cannot really comment on those. I can comment on the effects they have had on him though. Just verbalizing some of the incidents that he endured had noticeable effects on him, which I witnessed firsthand. Some of these are still evident long afterwards. A lot of the details were left out, and only now do I know the whole story.

I knew my husband's schedule, and when he was supposed to roll into bed, snuggle up next to me, and fall fast asleep. One morning when I awoke and realized he wasn't lying next to me; my heart skipped a beat. I immediately texted him, but there was no response. I texted again about ten minutes later, no response. I was constantly looking at our front door half expecting to hear a knock, and see one of his fellow officers with dreaded news.

Finally, after about an hour I heard the familiar jingle of his keys. A sigh of relief. He walked in the door, well, limped into the house was more like it. Apparently, he got into an altercation with a bad guy, punched him in the face, body slammed him into a wall, and in the process tweaked his ankle. Hey, thanks knucklehead bad guy for making me almost have a heart-attack.

All I remember is my husband saying, "You should see the other guy." Proud trooper wife moment. At least the bad guy didn't mess up my man's pretty face. That wasn't the only time he was late and I was a worried mess.

While he was working undercover there were nights when his phone would ring in the wee dark hours of the night. I distinctly remember two of these nights. One was to re-spond to a meth fire. He rolled out of bed, kissed me, and told me he was gonna bring home some extra bacon. That would have been great had I liked bacon. I know, I know, it's so un-American to dislike bacon. Anyways, the second occasion was to remove a device that is used for, let's just say, keeping track of certain things or people. That one re-ally worried me. I'll keep the details to myself and just let you use your imagination.

This book isn't about me or what I have experienced on a different side. This is why my section is so short. Maybe someday I'll relay all my life experiences and we can make this a series! Watch out *50 Shades of Grey*.

This book is written by my adoring husband as a way to record some of his career highs and lows, not only for our children, but possibly to help those who are wanting a ca-reer in law enforcement.

I would like to sincerely thank all of our police personnel across our wonderful country for your duty and sacrifice.

Trooper's Wife Out.

Chapter Eighteen

AMERICA WITHOUT POLICE OFFICERS

THE U.S. CONSTITUTION

I admit that for far too long, I was rather unfamiliar with the U.S. Constitution. Public school covered the subject lightly, as one might read a newspaper article. Officers swear an oath to uphold and defend the Constitution. We should probably be familiar with what we swear oaths to.

During the academy there were classes on how police work relates to the rights afforded to U.S. citizens, as described in the Constitution. This is of particular relevance for law enforcement officers, as agents of government; whether they work at the local, state, or federal level. The fourth and fifth amendments, impose significant boundaries on police, regarding their interactions with the public.

Our founding fathers, and their fathers before them, had long experienced what life was like apart from such rights. The government in England was oppressive. There were no restraints upon government entities, and citizens were subject to the everchanging, and overreaching whims of those in power.

What happens when people do not have the right to remain silent, protecting them from involuntary self-incrimination? They can be tortured into confessing anything, even if they are completely innocent.

When citizens do not have a right to privacy, explicitly from the government, every detail of their personal lives can be exposed to the view of the state. Such a level of government oversight could be used for political and religious persecution and oppression. The pages of history proliferate with examples of governments abusing power.

Unchecked centralized government power
is the single greatest plague upon humanity in history.

It is not in the pages of medical journals or physician manuals where we will find the entity with the highest death-toll. That contemptible record belongs to the governments of men. The U.S. Constitution, exists because of this. It was designed specifically to keep our government from becoming tyrannical. The authors of *A Patriot's History of the United States*, provide helpful insight on this:

> "In retrospect, they (the Bill of Rights) more accurately should be known as *the Bill of Limitations on government* to avoid the perception that the rights were granted by the government in the first place."

The first and second amendments are hot topics in the twenty-first century. America as we know it would cease to exist apart from each of these interdependent amendments. As the second protects the first, so also the first defends the second.

Police officers are charged with the mission of upholding the laws of the state and federal governments, primary among these stands the United States Constitution and the

Bill of Rights. Law enforcement officers are called upon to protect us from the lawless, so also, they are commissioned to defend our freedom.

"Concentrated power
has always been the enemy of liberty."
- Ronald Reagan

ANOTHER SEPARATION OF POWERS

Interestingly enough, America's law enforcement agencies have formed a unique version of a governmental separation of powers. Local, state, and federal agencies can each operate independently of the others. Thankfully we do not have one American police force. Rather, we have a conglomeration of nearly innumerable law enforcement agencies spread throughout our country. This is a healthy system, which inherently produces a suitable environment for checks and balances. While our system is not perfect, it is among the premier organizational structures in the world.

IMPLICATIONS

Without law enforcement officers, America would rapidly dissolve into a third world country. The power vacuum would draw in the strongest and most vicious. Like many nations around the world, we would become an environment of every man for himself, or one ruled by a violent totalitarian regime. Without restraint, the governments of men become tyrannical.

Make no mistake,
law enforcement in America
stands between peace and complete chaos.

In the last century alone history has recorded many such cases: as in Hitler's Germany, Stalin's Russia, and Mao's

China. It has been estimated that in the last one hundred years alone, well over 100,000,000 people have been murdered by their own governments. The three nations mentioned above account for at least half of that number, if not two thirds.

To give that number some perspective: It is estimated that the Germans massacred 6,000,000 Jews, during the Holocaust. That is more than the present combined population of Chicago, Dallas, Indianapolis, and Nashville.[13]

RECIPE FOR TYRANNY

I have travelled to several third-world countries (not tourist areas). It was shocking to see gun turrets at gas stations, armed guards at hotels, and military run airports. These were places where it was every man for himself. The police and military are largely corrupt and are often more to be concerned about than local gangs. I have witnessed firsthand what the world looks like with unchecked government power and without the freedoms that we enjoy in the States. Tyranny reigns over a massive portion of the earth.

There are mechanisms in place in the U.S. which presently keeps such tyranny at bay. However, these systems of government restraint are not invincible. In fact, they are remarkably susceptible to fracturing beneath the weight of too much power.

Consider all of the crime and violence in the daily news headlines throughout our country. What would happen if there were no one to address these issues? Who would keep chaos at bay? What would happen in America without police officers?

Freedom is worth any cost.
- John Adams, 1776

---

[13] http://worldpopulationreview.com

My name isn't C. K. Roberts,
but you can call me
Trooper.

SIXTY. TRIPLE. OUT.

Disclaimer

The accounts of police experiences contained herein are not in any way intended in to be a type of instruction manual for law enforcement. These incidents are presented as reports of events, not as recommended action.

Officers must always use discretion, and make the best decisions they can, given the situation and the information available to them at the time. Law enforcement entails response to a vast array of dangerous situations. Actions taken are ultimately the responsibility of the officer involved.

The lessons which I have learned during my career may not be appropriate for other officers, in their own particular circumstances. This information is merely experiential in nature. It has been disseminated as such, and is not suggested action or instructions.

Just because I have experience in this field, is not meant to indicate that I am an expert; because I am not. A few references to courage have been made in the narratives. Yet that does not mean that officers should put their lives in danger only because it would appear courageous to do so. A totality of the circumstances involved should always be considered. Occasionally courage looks like what it is, but in some situations, it may be complete foolishness. Knowing the difference calls for discretion.

It is my hope that police officers will use good judgment and exercise proper caution during the course of their duties. Wise officers will heed their training, and do what is necessary to be safe and return home at the end of their shift.

MSP Issues / External Documents

I have attached only a few supporting documents in the paperback version. The size of most of the others are too large to be legible in this format.

The external documents provided here include some pages from *Michigan State Police Issues*. This is a daily, statewide report of MSP noteworthy activity. While the *Issues* reports provided, include my activity, they also include reports of incidents involving other troopers from all over the state.

I had saved some of these *Issues* reports in a paper file, thinking that someday it might prove interesting to my children. Some of the others I was able to obtain in e-format. This accounts for the differences in appearances.

A few pages of *Issues* reports, which have been attached, refer to my cases, that have not been included in this project. Thus, I have left a bit of mystery for those interested in exercising their deduction abilities.

All of the names of the MSP personnel and dates, in each of the external reports have been redacted. This is in respect for the anonymity of these troopers and investigative teams.

Additional Documents

E-Book Version

The e-book version includes additional *Issues* documents, letters of appreciation from victims and prosecutors. A few of the letters refer to some of the reports involving the collaboration of several officers.

I have also included one page of statistics from one of my years of service (the pen marks are from a supervisor). This adds some weight to my prior statements regarding the volume of arrests which officers are involved in throughout their careers. This particular document also presents an example some of the various ways in which police officers serve society. Finally, I've included a copy of my retirement letter.

The purpose of presenting these documents is to authenticate many of the included narratives, and contribute to the overall credibility of this publication. I can attest to the validity of each record. They are all independently verifiable, as are each of the incidents recorded here.

"A PROUD tradition of SERVICE through
EXCELLENCE, INTEGRITY, and COURTESY"

CERTIFICATE OF RETIREMENT

To all whom it may concern

Tpr. ▮▮▮▮▮▮▮▮▮▮

having completed ▮▮▮▮▮ years of honorable and
faithful service as an enlisted member of the

MICHIGAN STATE POLICE

is hereby placed on retirement upon personal
request and in accordance with the provisions of the
Michigan State Police Retirement Law.

Director

Date of Retirement: ▮▮▮▮

217

█████,

Thank you. Now it is time for you to get ready for trial █████. ██, 20██.

I'll bet you never thought 2 kilos and a confession could be this much trouble.

10-█-2██

Briefs

STAFF REPORTS

███████ TOWNSHIP

Driver in snowmobile wreck hospitalized

███████████ 37, of ███████ remained in critical condition Sunday night after a snowmobile accident Friday at 11:37 p.m. on ████████ near ████████ Road in ████████ Township.

A second driver, ████████ 38, of ████████ was not injured ████ was transported to ████ Hospital, █ Alcohol was believed to be a factor in the accident, and an investigation is pending by the Michigan State Police █ Post.

The ███████ Township Police Department assisted at the scene.

███████████ TOWNSHIP

Troopers seize $50,000 in cocaine

A Michigan State Police trooper seized 2 kilograms of cocaine Sunday after a routine traffic stop in the eastbound lanes of Interstate ██ according to a news release from the █████ Post.

The drugs have an estimated street value of about $50,000, according to law enforcement officials.

The trooper arrested the 24-year-old driver and a 21-year-old passenger, both of Chicago. They face federal narcotics trafficking charges, Michigan state police said in the release.

███████████

Teenager reports rape by acquaintance

A 17-year-old ████████ girl told police Saturday she was raped by an acquaintance at the home of one of her relatives on ████████ Avenue, according to a police report.

The girl said she and the man were watching movies when the rape occurred.

The incident remains under investigation.

20-year-old reports attempted robbery

A 20-year-old ████████ man was not injured when a man attempted to stab him and demanded money at about 8:30 p.m. Saturday, according to a police report.

The man told police he was a passenger in a vehicle that became stuck in the 500 block of ████████ The driver then pulled a knife and demanded the passenger give him money. The victim refused, and the driver cut the victim's coat with the knife.

219

Feb. ██ ██

Dear Sir; Tpr. ███████

I would like to thank you for
your help on this case and
services also your concern you
showed for my daughter and myself.

We appreciated it very much.
My prayers are continuing for your
safety also.

Thank you again

█████ & █████

220

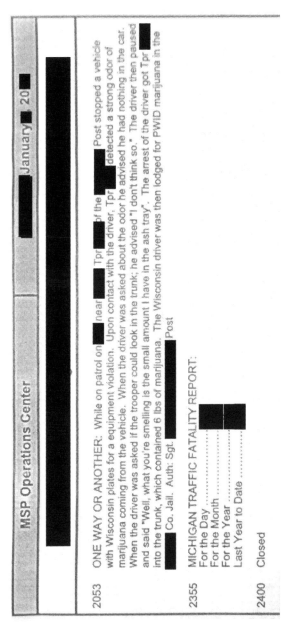

MSP Operations Center	January █, 20█

2053   ONE WAY OR ANOTHER: While on patrol on █ near █ Tpr █ of the █ Post stopped a vehicle with Wisconsin plates for a equipment violation. Upon contact with the driver, Tpr █ detected a strong odor of marijuana coming from the vehicle. When the driver was asked about the odor he advised he had nothing in the car. When the driver was asked if the trooper could look in the trunk; he advised "I don't think so." The driver then paused and said "Well, what you're smelling is the small amount I have in the ash tray". The arrest of the driver got Tpr █ into the trunk, which contained 6 lbs of marijuana. The Wisconsin driver was then lodged for PWID marijuana in the █ Co. Jail. Auth: Sgt. █ Post

2355   MICHIGAN TRAFFIC FATALITY REPORT:
For the Day ....
For the Month ....
For the Year ....
Last Year to Date ....

2400   Closed

SAFETY REMINDER From Governors Highway Safety Association (GHSA) Cells phones and Texting
In Michigan, teens with probationary licenses whose cell phone usage contributes to a traffic crash or ticket may not use
a cell phone while driving

B & E SOLVED Tpr ▮▮▮ was dispatched to a B&E / UDAA. The residence was that of a subject who passed away
within the last few days. Family members noticed the breaking and entering and vehicle theft. Tpr ▮▮▮ assisted
the investigation by contacting ▮▮▮ Discount and determining that a suspect had pawned off a gold ring, a knife, and
some coins. The suspect was identified the troopers located an address via SNAP. Located at that address was the
suspect who pawned the stolen items and another suspect who lived next door to the victimized residence. Additional
stolen property was located at the residence. One of the suspects confessed to Tpr ▮▮▮ regarding his part in the B&E /
vehicle theft and the sale of the stolen items. Suspect #2 confessed to Tpr ▮▮▮ regarding his part in the B&E
possessing pills taken from the victim's residence, and the location of the stolen vehicle which was promptly recovered
Excellent team work by the day shift.

AUTH F/Lt ▮▮▮ Post

222

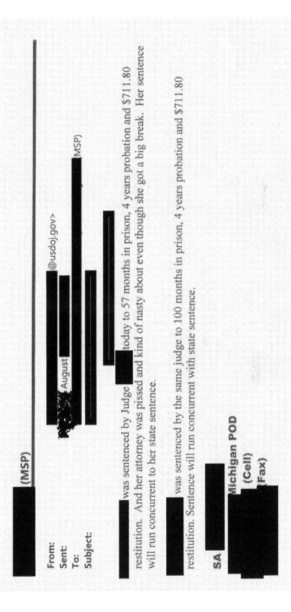

(MSP)

From: ████████████@usdoj.gov>
Sent: ████ August ████
To: ██████████ (MSP)
Subject: ██████████

████████ was sentenced by Judge ████████ today to 57 months in prison, 4 years probation and $711.80 restitution. And her attorney was pissed and kind of nasty about even though she got a big break. Her sentence will run concurrent to her state sentence.

████████ was sentenced by the same judge to 100 months in prison, 4 years probation and $711.80 restitution. Sentence will run concurrent with state sentence.

SA ████████
Michigan POD
██████ (Cell)
██████ (Fax)

Mothers Against Drunk Driving

MADD

Michigan State Organization

Certificate of Special Appreciation

Presented to

Trooper

for Outstanding Efforts in Drunk Driving Prevention and Law Enforcement

Date

MADD Michigan

MADD

Bibliography

Grossman, David. _On Combat_: _The Psychology and Physiology of Deadly Conflict in War and in Peace_. Killology Research Group. 2012.

McCullough, David. _1776_. New York: Simon & Shuster. 2005.

Schweikart & Allen, _A Patriot's History of the United States_, New York: Sentinel. 2014.

Van Der Kolk, Bessel. _The Body Keeps Score_. New York: Penguin Books. 2014.

Van Horne, Patrick, and Riley, Jason. _Left of Bang: How the Marine Corps' Combat Hunter Program Can Save Your Life_. New York: Black Irish Entertainment LLC. 2014.